"Sculling in a Nutshell is fantastic! The analogies are delightful and humorous and offer perfect 'snap-shots' for athletes to reference throughout the stroke. Gordon's passion for the sport and understanding of boat dynamics jump off the pages. A profound instructional guide for all levels."

Saiya Remmler— Silver Medal, LW2X World University Games, 1989; Bronze Medal, Ltw. World Championships, LW2X with Teresa Zarzeczny Bell, 1992; 4th LW2X, World Championships with Lindsay Burns, 1993; Head of the Charles Results: Gold Medal, Championship W2X with Teresa Zarzeczny Bell (course record), 1992; 5 x Gold Medal, Masters W2X with Teresa Zarzeczny Bell, 2007-2011 (current course record).)

"Gordon is a "one percenter" among rowing coaches with an uncanny ability to accelerate learning. Like all good coaches, he clearly explains what needs to be done. What sets him apart from the rest is the way he conveys how to improve technique, and why each move is important."

Chuck Cook—Masters National G1X ltwt. Champion 2009, 2010—11. Other Championship Medals—2007-2011

"Sculling in a Nutshell is an elegant, complete and beautiful study. Immerse yourself in the functional nuts and bolts of rowing technique, as well as sharing Hamilton's evident delight in the graceful nutshell itself that is the rowing stroke. Within lies a path to understanding, opportunities to practice and perfect, and above all to share in Hamilton's love of the graceful artistry of rowing."

Kat Astley — Stroke of Cambridge University Woman's Boat Club (CUWBC) winning Blue Boat against Oxford, 1997 & , President of CUWBC, 1998, Coach for Cambridge University Woman's Boat Club, 2002-2009 Coach/Boatman, Christ's College, Cambridge University 2006-2009

SCULLING IN

A Polemical Guide to Making Your Boat Go Faster

A NUTSHELL

Gordon Hamilton

SCULLING (AND SWEEPING) WITH STABILITY AND EASE

ScullNut X books

A good general rule is to think of yourself as a piece of the equipment. The law of Stability is: If you are not stable, you are not stable. Or, as one wise Florida Rowing Center sculler, Eugene Van Loan, put it, "If you are not stable, you are not able."

Sculling in a Nutshell
ISBN 978-0-615-67956-3
Cover Photograph of rowers Teresa Zarzeczny Bell
and Saiya Remmler by Ann Robbart
Illustrations by Giselle Hunter-Ensor and Alicia Kelly
Editing by Eugene Van Loan III

Contents

Acknowledgements

There have been many people who have had an enormous impact on my coaching and the circumstances which have led to the production of this book — I hope you will see yourselves in these pages and accept my gratitude. Of these people, I would particularly like to recognize:

Rachel Jackson, Pete Peterson and Ann Robbart.

Florida Rowing Center Partners: Bob Wolfe, Ken Iscol, Duck Wadsworth. Coaches Marlene Royle, Harvey Rubenstein, Bob Van Twyver and Allen Rosenberg. My editor Eugene Van Loan III, graphic designer Christopher Burg, and illustrators Giselle Hunter-Ensor and Alicia Kelly.

My wife Roberta and son Rusty and Judy, my mother-in-law, because…

Introduction

Taking his inspiration from Steve Fairbairn, the famous Australian Rowing Coach of the early 20th century who did most of his coaching at Cambridge University, Gordon brings a refreshing perspective based upon sound theory and common sense with a bit of counter-intuitive instruction thrown in.

While many books on rowing claim to be written for all levels, this one surely is, and for sweeps as well as sculling. Though it is written mostly from a sculler's perspective, the principles apply equally to both.

Following Fairbairn's ideas, Gordon, rightly, puts a large emphasis on how to make your boat stable and therefore preserve the momentum of the shell during the recovery. These are invaluable insights.

Those new to the sport will gain a critical understanding of the fundamentals of the rowing stroke. Those of an intermediate level will discover new ways to think about things; and elite scullers will learn some new perspectives, be reminded of some things they may have forgotten and be "re-introduced" to some things they did not know they knew.

Gordon calls this book a polemic because he is making a case for a particular point of view. In some cases this point of view sounds very, very different from what many other coaches will tell you. He is "old school" with a twist.

This is a book to be read over and over again!

As Gordon says — "The proof is in the puddle."

— Roger Silk Cambridge, England

Roger Silk was a full time rowing coach for Lady Margaret Boat Club, St. John's College, Cambridge University for over 40 years. From 1984 to 2009 he was Head Coach to Cambridge University Women's Boat Club. In 2007, he received a lifetime award from the Amateur Rowing Association of the U.K. in recognition for his long and lasting contribution to coaching. During his career, Roger has sent numerous women to the GB National Squad.

Preface

There are a variety of ways to work towards improving your sculling and gaining boat-speed and many very good coaches will approach this from different perspectives. Sometimes you may hear the exact opposite of what is written here.

After all the training, all the sweat and the tears of joy and tears of sorrow, in the end your increased speed and sculling improvement is going to come from the brief time during the entry of the blade into the water while the blade is still moving, being "sucked", toward the finish line before the blade's tip begins to arc around toward the stern of your shell.

While lift and drag forces are working on the blades throughout the entire time they are in the water, it is this brief moment when your blades get "locked on" and "held and pulled" by the water that will make the most difference. If executed properly, instead of creating all the violence and turbulence and wasted energy we see so often, you will be working with the water rather than against it ("feeling the water").

This is the case, whether you are approaching your prime, in your prime, or on the other side of the hill. Nobody has speed to waste. And since nobody is getting younger, nobody has time to waste.

How, then, do you develop the poise at the entry to maximize this brief window of time when your blades are entering and being loaded by the water? How do you avoid the sense of desperation, chance and free fall that people often feel when they try to place the blades in the water? How can you develop the patience to allow the blade to get "locked on", to find that golden mean between caution and desperate abandon?

In short, the key is STABILITY. And how do you become stable? The answer is quite simple: learn to become one with your boat as if you were a piece of the equipment.

And, if there is one key thing, one idea that will improve your sculling more than anything, it is the ability to keep your weight off your feet during the Recovery until AFTER the blade is loaded and locked on.

At any time during the Recovery, as soon as your weight is on the foot stretcher, the boat begins to slow down rapidly. But perhaps we are getting ahead of ourselves. There are reasons for every movement you do and they are all intended to make it easier to improve your stability and therefore speed. The execution of these movements requires some basic techniques, knowledge and lots of practice. **The theme of Sculling in a Nutshell is to give you an explanation of what you should do during the stroke, how you should do it and why you should do it this way.**

Release and Follow-Through

Chapter **1**

While we like to think (and many have been told by coaches) that there is neither beginning nor end to the rowing stroke, this is not true. It all begins with the Release and Follow-Through. It is from here that everything else follows.

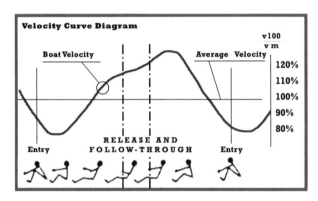

The **curve of velocity** in the diagram demonstrates the **velocity variation** of the **boat** during **one stroke** in relation to the average velocity.

The objective at all times is for you to become one with your boat. This is especially true at the Release. To do this, you must engage your frame (core through arms) with the frame of the boat (riggers through pins).

This engagement of your frame to the frame of the boat is analogous to the embrace of ballroom dancers. The communication between the leader and the follower takes place through the embrace, especially the elbows. Any looseness either in the leader's or in the follower's elbows results in jerky, sudden movements (and often a change of partners at the end of the dance). You can know all the steps but if the embrace is poor you cannot dance! The connection of your frame and the frame of the boat is just as important.

At the back end of the Drive, beginning with the Release, you must make yourself into a Fortress of Stability. Your hands should be on as close to the same plane as possible and your elbows should be angled out from your sides in front of your body, pushing through the elbows firmly into the blades.

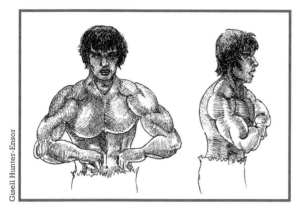

Gisell Hunter-Ensor

Hulk

Note shoulders are not **"hunched"**. They are **"rolled"** **forward** naturally as the elbows remain in front of your core. The shoulders must maintain this rolled forward position **throughout the entire stroke!** This keeps the shoulder girdle stable and your major back muscles **engaged**.

The elbows should be in front of your core and the shoulders down and "rolled" toward the handles.

To get a sense of what this should feel like, place your elbows at your sides with your forearms parallel to the floor. Now rotate your elbows out and forward until they are in front of your belly. Notice how your shoulders naturally roll forward, following your elbows and upper arms.

This rolling of the shoulders down and forward stabilizes your shoulder girdle and therefore your upper arms and elbows so that you can "hinge" the forearms down, such that you can extract the blade without the elbows and upper arms moving. This is very important in order to be connected to your boat as if you were a piece of the equipment.

The elbows are the forgotten body part of the rowing stroke!

For example, if you were to leave the dock with a loose rigger which jiggled during the Release, you would rightly feel that you could not row this boat, and you would return to the dock to tighten the rigger. Allowing your elbows to move or shift has the same effect as a loose rigger. When the elbows shift, you are disconnected from the riggers, pins, and boat, essentially in free fall. This is often why a sculler's release is sloppy, with the blade wrestled out of the water, and the shell unstable.

Keep a "vertical orientation" with your weight above your hands, pushing the elbows into the pins, with your navel "drawn into your spine" and lifting yourself from your belly and chest. Your shoulder blades should feel as though they were glued to your back rib cage and down ("in your back pocket"). The shoulders should be rolled forward. Keep your shoulders from rising up and do not allow your elbows to fall below your hands.

As mentioned, just as you learn when properly learning to do crunches, or in yoga class, you should have your navel drawn into your spine, relieving tension in your lower back. You should hold this "drawn-in-to-the-spine" position throughout the entire stroke. **You are now a Fortress of Stability and ready to execute the Release.**

Release the blade from the water when the backs of your knees hit the seat deck at the end of the Drive, and before the handles have come so far back as to hit your body. Hinge the forearms down without moving the elbows from their horizontal plane (which are in front of your belly).

This motion is very similar to how you would lift yourself out of a swimming pool with your hands on the pool deck pointing towards each other and your elbows out/forward and stable through stabilizing your shoulder girdle by rolling the shoulders forward and down. You engage through your core and press through your elbows. (Rock climbers call this "Mantling"). However, if even one of your elbows wiggles, you are going to be slithering out of the pool, at best. Not what you would call a "stable" exit from the pool.

Do not feather the blade out of the water; come out square. This means that your wrists must remain flat at the extraction. After the Release, feather your blades using your knuckles rather than wrists. (See notes on Feathering)

While keeping your trunk still and bracing your trunk and legs, after the Release, use the energy of the Drive and simply change the direction of the oar handles as though you were, in the words of Allen Rosenberg, releasing a Frisbee, allowing the handles to swing away without effort. I

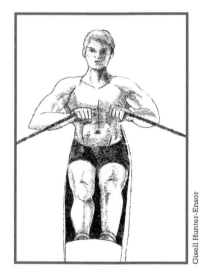

Keep your **elbows** on the **same horizontal plane** during **Release** and **Follow-Through**.

Gisell Hunter-Ensor

call this the Follow-Through. It is extremely important to keep the elbows on the same horizontal plane as the forearms are hinging down and then extending out during the Follow-Through. (Note: when releasing a Frisbee, with a back hand toss, the forearm hinges down and extends out while the elbow remains on the same horizontal plane.)

Use your elbows to send the handles away and to keep pressure on the pins in the direction that the blade is moving. As Steve Fairbairn put it, "Try to squeeze the button through the rowlock at each end of the stroke". Slowly Forward, Notes on Rowing: The Complete Steve Fairbairn On Rowing, Pp. 533. This is done by using the muscles of your core and arms, especially your triceps. Not the Thumbs! Pressure from the thumbs should be just enough to hold your hand on the end of the oar, to prevent it from sliding down the handle.

Do not rest at the release! Rest after this follow through with your hands away and the body over.

Suggested Drills:

- King of the Mountain (#1)
- Square Blades Rowing (#13)
- Feet-Out (#10)

Follow-Through and Recovery

Chapter **2**

The main focus of the Recovery is to maintain your connection to your boat while gliding forward into the Entry, and to establish stability with your blades off the water. This stable oneness with your boat brings you to the Entry with poise and as much effective length as possible without causing violence to the run of the boat (preserving the momentum). This oneness between you and your boat is physical just like the oneness between the rigging and the boat. However, because you are a sentient being, you must be careful to not over-think things. This requires some willingness to "just let go." **Let the boat be a boat—let it float!**

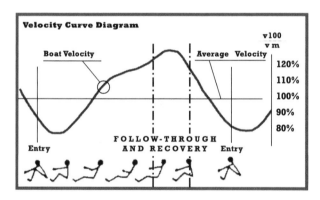

Note slight increase of speed of shell as the hands **swing away** and the body **rocks over**.

The Recovery should be 100% upper body. During the entire process, the legs and hips must be as relaxed and removed from any tension as possible. This means you do not want to use them to pull yourself and the seat into the stern or "draw" the shell under you. (see Skimming Drill #4)

Make your frame the frame of the boat; imagine that you are a child on a jungle gym, supported by your elbows on the frame of the jungle gym, letting your legs and hips swing freely while your upper body is stable and solid. The riggers are your jungle gym. **Your entire core/frame, especially the large muscles of your back, is engaged in this.**

Or, if you have downhill skiing experience, picture yourself among the moguls. Your upper body/core is stable while the hips remain relaxed and the legs follow the skis. Any effort to direct the skis and you will wipe out. Any collapse of your core stability and you will wipe out.

Another mental image that might be helpful is the gymnast performing what is known as the Iron Cross on the rings. His outstretched arms are one with the rings, just as yours must be with the riggers, and his lower

The riggers are your jungle gym.
Make your frame the frame of the boat.
Have fun!

body hangs free, just as yours should. Note how the gymnast engages his entire core/frame, especially the large muscles of his back, in order to suspend himself above the rings. You must do the same in order to hold yourself above the riggers and to maintain your mechanical connection to them, i.e., with your elbows and stable shoulder girdle.

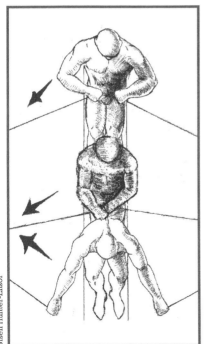

After the Release and during the Follow-Through, it is essential that one's hands follow as close a pattern of self-similarity on the same plane as possible. The motion of the hands as you extract the blades should be down, parallel to your belly, then sternward, parallel to your thighs as the arms begin to extend, and then once there is no longer a danger of hitting your knees, parallel to the water.

Force Vectors

Not the Thumbs! Transfer your core strength into the pins in the direction the blades are moving—**through your elbows.**

10

Follow-Through and Recovery

Use your elbows to send the handles away and to keep pressure on the pins in the direction that the blade is moving. This is done by using the muscles of your core and arms, especially your triceps. Not the Thumbs! Pressure from the thumbs should be just enough to hold your hand on the end of the oar, to prevent it from sliding down the handle.

Because of the geometry of the rigging, the fact that the oar handles crossover/overlap as they swing away on the Follow-Through (and on the Drive as well, for that matter), the elbows necessarily come in closer together, that is pull away from the pins, as the arms begin to straighten. This path of the elbows during the Follow-Through is one of the most critical yet least attended to parts of the stroke. Full attention is required to avoid your elbows dropping or losing your pressure into the pin/blade as the arms begin to swing away. (see King of the Mountain Drill #1)

Remember, any movement of the elbows from their horizontal plane, any movement which removes your frame from that of the boat, will have the same effect as having your riggers loose. Again, think of yourself as a piece of the equipment—**be the boat!**

The arms swing out easily, following the energy of the Drive. Keep your sternum up and trunk still by lifting from your belly and chest and drawing your latissimus dorsi muscles (lats) down onto the riggers. Keep the elbows engaged and pushing into the pins in the direction the blades are moving.

The "orthodox" pattern of the hands coming away out of bow is to have the left hand lead slightly ahead of the right; however, it does not make much difference if you lead with your left or right hand. Most sculling boats in this country (U.S.A.) and Europe are rigged with the left (starboard) oarlock slightly higher than the right (port). The left hand will be "stacked" on top of the right. This is done so that the hands will not collide with each other as they come to the "crossover" (overlap) point of the Recovery.

However, I feel that it is much better in terms of symmetry and stability to have the hands on as close to the same plane as possible with one leading the other out on the Recovery and following it in on the Drive. As the left hand leads the right out of the bow, the space between your second and third, the largest, knuckle of the right hand should brush against the base of the thumb of the leading left hand. It is useful to make this gentle contact so that you have the tactile reinforcement of your symmetry. If you are able to set your oarlocks at the same height, do so.

After the Release, as the arms are swinging away with the knees relaxed but gently held down, make a commitment to get your hands low enough to keep your blades off the water. While first learning to scull, it is comforting to let the blades skim along the surface of the water, believing that this aids your stability. In fact, the blades bouncing along on any waves are actually removing your frame from the boat, putting your attention into your hands, which are bouncing up and down. In short, the blades on the water are destabilizing your shell and preventing you from ever becoming one with your boat and letting the boat properly float and truly run. Additionally, it makes rowing in rough water very unpleasant, if not impossible.

During the Recovery, keep your weight off your feet. This means keep pressure off the foot stretcher up to and through the placement of the blade into the water and its loading! This will allow you to feel as though it is the water which is "loading the feet" after the Entry. If at any time during the Recovery you allow your weight to settle on the foot stretcher, the boat will slow down—rapidly.

So, I repeat—keep the weight off your feet on the Recovery!

When first learning this technique of applying pressure against the pins in the direction that your blades are moving, it is necessary to exaggerate the pressure to recognize the feeling. As Fairbairn urges, try to "squeeze" the button of the oar through the oarlock! This is, of course, an exaggeration.

Ultimately, we are after "relaxed firmness", somewhat as though one were standing at attention. You can stand at attention for hours if you preserve your structural integrity through this relaxed firmness. As soon as you let yourself "relax" without this "firmness", your weight settles into one place, (for example, your left knee, or your right knee, or whatever) and then you get into trouble. So, as practitioners of the martial arts might say, you want to temper rigidity with flexibility as if you were " a stalk of bamboo".

Another way of looking at this is similar to what is known in the Alexander Technique as "standing with poise"; that is, your spine/skeletal system distributes your weight throughout your body. Similarly, when you connect your frame to the riggers, you are distributing your weight throughout the entire boat, not localizing it on the seat or feet. By using "relaxed firmness" to engage your skeletal system with the skeletal system of the boat (through the riggers), you are distributing your weight throughout the boat and creating a sort of structural integrity between sculler and machine.

And, if you do this correctly, you will feel as though you are riding the riggers into the stern, all the way into the Entry—**because you are keeping your weight off your feet**.

Remember, any movement of the elbows, any movement which removes your frame from that of the boat will have the same effect as having your riggers loose. Again, think of yourself as a piece of the equipment. **Be The Boat!**

The arms swing out easily, following the energy of the Drive. Keep your sternum up and trunk still by lifting from your belly and chest and drawing your latissimus dorsi muscles (lats) down onto the riggers. Keep the elbows engaged and pushing into the pins in the direction the blades are moving.

■ Reach and Body Preparation Phase of the Recovery ■

We said above that if the rowing stroke has a beginning, it begins with the Release. From there we transition through the Recovery to the Entry. We have already discussed how the Recovery is initiated with the Follow-Through. Another way of thinking about this initial phase of the Recovery is to describe it as the Reach and Body Preparation Phase.

Because of the difficulty of maintaining pressure against the pins in the direction of the blades as the elbows come inward towards each other while the arms are extending during the Follow-Through, I advocate separating the acts of the arms swinging away from the body (the Reach, or Follow-Through) from the torso itself rocking over (the Preparation of the Body). This is because it is simply more difficult to feel your frame connected to the frame of the boat if both arms and body are coming out of bow together.

After the Reach, begin the Body Preparation by releasing your knees, allowing them to crack up just slightly, and rotating your pelvis, making sure not to lose the pressure against the pins through your core and elbows. It is important to release the knees because the main muscles which rotate your pelvis are the quadriceps and the lower abdominals. While there is nothing wrong with "lock-

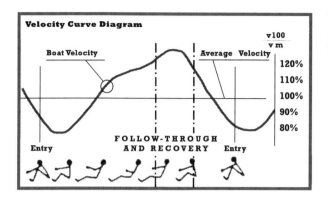

There is a **nice boost of speed** as the body **rocks over.**

ing your knees" at the very back end of the Drive because this helps with your connection to the pins, if the knees are "locked" now, this rotation of your pelvis is much less fluid. (See Swan Drill #6)

If you look at your velocity curve, you see that there is a nice boost in the acceleration of the shell just as the body rocks over. This is the result of Newton's Third Law of Motion which states that for every action there is an equal and opposite reaction. This is another reason for separating the swinging away of the oar handles from the torso rocking over. Become sensitive to this. You will first hear the sound of bubbles running along the side of the hull and then gradually become aware of the feel of the boat accelerating. **Cultivate this!**

The full arm extension and the full body angle must be accomplished before the seat begins to move into the stern (see Skimming Drill). However, be careful not to reach so far as to pull the shoulders out of their sockets or the shoulder blades off the rear of your rib cage. The whole feeling should be one of connection to the boat by lifting the belly and chest and drawing the lats down onto the riggers, thereby keeping your weight off your feet and distributing it throughout the shell. Again, think of "riding the riggers".

In geometric terms, we can think of the Reach and Body Preparation Phase as establishing the radius of a circle. In the next phase, the Length Phase, the hands and arms trace a path along the circumference of that circle.

Suggested Drills:

- Skimming (#4)
- Rock and Row (#3)

This completes the Reach/Body Preparation Phase.

■ Length and Entry Phase of the Recovery ■

After establishing your Reach and Body Preparation without the
seat moving, you now begin to establish the "Length" of your Recovery. As
you move up the slide, this will eventually lead you to the Entry and the
commencement of the Drive.

This should be accomplished without pulling yourself forward with your
legs. Your movement into the stern comes from the continuous separation of
the handles from your core as you continue to apply pressure backwards towards the bow against the pins through the elbows. Imagine you are sitting
on a giant skateboard with your hands on the sides of pocket doors that slide
into the doorframe. In our construct, these doors are the riggers/pins. Now
propel yourself through the doorway by pushing out and back towards the
blades (which are moving further and further behind you) by separating the
elbows/arms. The legs are not necessary for this, and, in fact, any tension in
them will only create difficulties at the Entry.

In addition, it is important to continue lifting your weight off the feet and
staying light on the seat by drawing the lats down and "resting" your weight
on the riggers through the elbows. Keep your core firm, body angle set and
arms loose, but straight; continue pushing the handles apart. All the while,
apply pressure against the pins toward the blades through the elbows.
Continue this through the immersion of the blade into the water and
the transition into the Drive.

Make every effort to have your hands as close as possible to the same
plane and to keep them in this relative position. The symmetry of the hands
while your trunk and arm muscles are applying pressure against the pins
and the drawing down of your major back muscles will not only stabilize
your body, but it will stabilize your shell. If you find the shell down to one
side, leave it there and make the correction at the Release of the following
Drive. Be particularly assiduous in making your Release at the correct point
(see Drive) and keeping pressure on the pins and making symmetrical
patterns as the hands swing away.

While drawing yourself into the stern by applying pressure against the pins
in the direction that the blades are moving, there is no need to think in terms
of "slide control." If your legs and hips are relaxed and you are supporting
your body on the rigger frame by applying constant pressure against the
pins, you are not "controlling" the boat; you are becoming part of it. **It is
you and you are it**.

A mong other things, the notion of "control" will tense your legs. This in turn will only serve to centralize your weight onto the foot stretcher and begin to check the boat, slowing its speed.

Using the legs to draw yourself forward will create timing issues at the Entry, especially in team boats. When you are moving with the shell (as felt by constant pressure on the pins through the elbows) in a sense of neutrality relative to the movement of the shell, your only issue becomes being "On Time." You do not have to be "fast" or "slow", early or late, just on time...with the boat.

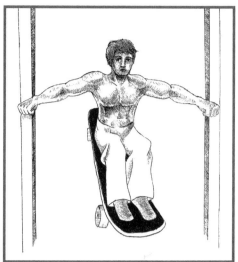

Draw yourself **through** the pocket doors **without** using **your legs** to pull yourself forward. The **Recovery** is **100% upper body**.

Gisell Hunter-Ensor

When you and the boat are connected through the "embrace" of your frame with the frame of the boat, you have all the time you need to do everything that needs to be done. Movements can be quick, as quick as the blink of the eye, and at the same time they can also be subtle and fluid. Looking at the velocity curve of a single stroke, one is struck by the beautiful smoothness of the fluctuations in its slope and amplitude. Motions should never be sudden! Boats do not respond to sudden. They seek out the path of least resistance. Sudden should be a huge red flag that something is desperately wrong.

■ Stability vs. Balance ■

During the Recovery, stabilize yourself! Do not attempt to "balance" the boat. Remember the jungle gym and moguls images. Allow the boat to float. In short, let it be a boat! The less you try to control the boat, to prevent it from rocking and rolling, the more stable it will become. And, think of being stable relative to the shell, not the water! In fact, during the Recovery, you want to make the water disappear. It is only your frame and the frame of the boat that matters.

When you were first introduced to rowing, you were probably taught to lift one hand and then the other and to note the effect this had on the "balance" of your shell. Unfortunately, this tends to give you the idea that you are supposed to balance the boat by this movement of your hands. Rather, the lesson should be that these are the very movements which destabilize the boat. However, if you internalized this unfortunate lesson, you have probably been chasing the elusive ghost called "balance" ever since.

Balance is a difficult concept. It is dynamic. Stability seems much simpler, more approachable. In a rowing shell, balance only makes sense to me within the context of Stability. Stability comes about by keeping constant pressure against the pins in the direction the blades are moving while making consistent symmetrical patterns with the hands/handles. It comes from making yourself stable with your core, supported through your elbows into the riggers. When you keep the pressure on the pins, you widen the shell out to the pins. The boat becomes over 5 feet wide. However, when we focus on balance, especially by using your hands or your feet or by wiggling about on your seat, you shrink the shell into a narrow needle that becomes a problem to set.

There are some people who can naturally "balance" a boat, just as there are always about 1% of the people who participate in any sport who can just do it. Stability is for the rest of us! It is the symmetry of your movements and the steadiness of your upper body which will create stability. Once you have learned how to stabilize your shell, balance will not matter. **"Balance" is a word I would like to consign to the Lexicon of Bad Rowing.**

■ Constant pressure against the Pin ■

This is one of the main themes of the Nutshell. Using the friction between the outside of your hands and the handle, your forearms, your triceps, your pectoral muscles, your lats, and your entire core, you should be applying pressure into the pins through stable elbows.

However, **do not use your thumbs!** Your thumbs are not designed for this type of work. They rest on the face of the handle to let you know where the end of the oar is. The only pressure you need to apply with your thumbs is just enough to prevent your hands from sliding down the oar handles while the hands themselves remain "soft".

Many of us learned to row being told that we should be applying "lateral pressure." We are now simply taking this notion a bit further, and taking it much more seriously. The pressure we are looking for is always applied in a specific vector, which is directed toward the blade. Imagine that your eyeballs are on your elbows and that they are always "looking" at the blades. Consequently, at the Release, you are pressing toward the stern where the blades are finishing the Drive. At mid-Recovery, where the blades are perpendicular to the shell, the vector is indeed lateral, and at the Entry, where the blades are engaging the water, it is toward the bow. (See Vector Illustration pp10.)

During the Recovery (and as we will see on the Drive), the force vector shifts and changes with the position of the blade. The stroke is never two dimensional, never "ergometer" rowing. We are not concerned with pushing or pulling the handles anywhere. We are always working in three dimensions, always working against the pins, applying pressure towards the blades.

It is enormously useful to picture this three dimensional movement in your mind's eye. Picture the changes in the direction of the force vector toward the blades as you move through the Recovery and during the Drive. Mentally embrace this idea while performing it.

At first, when just learning to take this seriously, you must exaggerate this notion. You will come in off the water with sore, tired triceps and, perhaps, pectoral muscles. You will say to yourself, "This cannot be right". And, you will be correct. We do not want to be wasting all that energy. We want what I call "relaxed firmness". Just as there is a difference between leaning against a wall trying to push your hand through the plaster and simply resting your weight against it such that if you removed your hand, you would fall, we ultimately want to simply be resting against the pins, using them for support. In the end, that is all you need. On the other hand, this is an acquired talent. If you begin with such "finesse", you will never learn when you are truly applying the type of pressure in the direction of the blade that we want. Push your hand through the wall at first, or as Fairbairn put it, try to push the button through the oarlock. (See Vector Illustration)

Suggested Drills:

■ Pause drills (#2) for symmetry of hand movements and body preparation and reinforcing the difference between the first phase of the Recovery and the second phase leading into the Entry.

■ "Skimming" (#4) for the movement into the stern without using your legs to draw yourself forward. Relaxing the hips and legs and keeping the hands/elbows separating while applying pressure against the pins in the direction the blades are moving.

■"Swans" (#6) to learn the proper rotation of the pelvis for correct body angle and posture.

The Entry

Chapter **3**

"There is no catch"

First, I think that the very word "catch" gives the totally wrong impression. Think Entry, not Catch. This is water we are talking about. You cannot catch it! Your goals are to let the water accept the blade and to work with the water, rather than against it. There is no post behind which we can set the blade and "lever" ourselves past, as many coaches say. We can deposit "catch" into the Lexicon of Bad Rowing, along with "balance".

If you must use the word "catch", think of it as referring to the moment when the tip of the blade begins to swing around toward the starting line (stern of your boat) and the handles come back towards you. In other words, when you begin the Drive. Not when the blade enters the water!

■ The Entry is the very last part of the Recovery ■

The Entry is what the Recovery is all about. It is as quick as a blink, subtle and quiet. It is the golden mean between caution and desperate abandon; its essence is Poise. It is the transition from the female principle of the Recovery (as follower) to the male principle of the Drive (as leader).

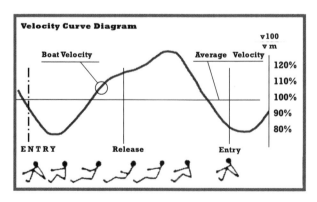

Note the continued **slowing down** of the shell during the **last part** of the **Recovery** and through the immersion of the blade into the water and the **beginning** of the **Drive. You are the cause of this!**

As Florida Rowing Center student, Wendy Lomicka observed, continuing the analogy of Ballroom Dancing from the very beginning of this book, as you move up the slide on the Recovery, drawing yourself through the pocket doors by separating your arms, leading into the Entry, you are creating a space into which you are inviting the stern of your boat to enter. **Stay out of the way. Keep off your feet through the Entry. Let the boat float. Let it run**.

There are only three options for the sequence of the Entry of the blade into the water vis-à-vis the motion of your body. Either you are still moving into the stern as the blade enters the water, or you have stopped your movement into the stern by pushing onto the foot stretcher as you make the Entry or, you are on the Drive as the blade enters. There are no other options. This is not quantum physics. **You cannot be moving in two directions at once. No "simultaneous" or "instantaneous" change of direction is possible**.

Suffice it to say that these three options are not created equal. The least preferred is the third, entering the water during the Drive. This is the classic case of "missing water" or "rowing the blades in." The second is not as pernicious, but still to be avoided. It will still be checking, slowing the shell, though not as much. Accordingly, the Entry should occur as your body is still moving towards the stern.

You need to be as stable at the Entry as you have been throughout the entire Recovery. As you approach the Entry, keep sitting up with your navel still drawn into our spine. Maintain that Fortress of Stability which you established at the Release.

Now comes the hard part. You must turn on its head how you probably have been taught to think of the Entry. In keeping with the idea of always applying pressure against the pins in the direction of the blades, do not make the Entry by thinking of swinging the hands "up and away," as if doing a swan dive. This will pull you off the pin, however slightly, and cause you to be unstable, as if in free fall, at the most critical of times. You will have to rely on the foot stretcher to break this fall and you will begin to check the speed of the shell. Continue to keep the oars moving parallel to the water and pretend that you are smoothing out a tablecloth until pushing the blades into the water.

Slightly open the angle of your armpits while pushing down and back against the pins towards the blade and keep very "soft hands". Push the blades into the water from your core rather than thinking of lifting the hands. While your hands continue to separate, squeeze your shoulder blades together and with the lats engaged, feel as though you are pushing your back through your shoulders (see back end of Drive as contrast). Feel as though you are "hoisting" your torso above the pins, rather than lifting your hands. Make sure that your elbows are still turned out (NOT DOWN) as they have been from your very first "Hulk/Mantle" posture. **Note: this also prevents you from breaking your elbows and pulling the handles with your biceps as you begin the Drive, something you, probably, do not want to do**.

With relaxed legs and a firm and steady bamboo-like core and your weight still off the foot stretchers, the process of "pushing" out and back against the pins (while still separating the handles) will continue to propel you and your seat into the stern even as the blades enter the water. Keep pressure against the pins by using your rhomboids through your elbows to push back towards the blades and use your core muscles to stabilize yourself and to separate the handles all the way through the Entry. Keeping your sternum up, feel as though you are expanding your chest while suspended on the riggers as you slice the blades into the water. You cannot allow yourself to fall off the pins onto the feet! Ride the riggers into the Entry, not the foot stretchers! In this way, you will be making the Entry while still on the Recovery.

If your hands remain soft and your core/elbows firmly and clearly connected to the pins, you can feel as though you are virtually throwing the blades into the water. Use your core muscles to make the Entry, not the hands. Your connection to the pins is from your core through the elbows, **not the hands**.

It is important to make the Entry with as little turbulence as possible. Do not announce the Entry. Do not think of "catching" anything! Allow the water to accept the blade. If you do this, once the blades are half buried, the water will grab them and pull them forward and toward the bow. If your hands are soft, this will cause the handles to be pulled gently into your finger tips.

You are not after a back-splash—you are after a simple Greg Louganis moment —a small "V" of water-displacement. It will sound like a pebble dropping into a still pond, almost a kiss, not a smack.

This is a gross motor operation involving much larger muscles than simply your hands. Our hands are way too clever. They do things we do not intend;

one hand may dominate, dip, rise, clutch or grab. They move at different speeds. Keep the Entry gross and simple, allowing the hands to be light and relaxed. Roughness in your hands will seriously interfere with your ability to feel the water and to work with the speed of the boat.

In the entire rowing stroke sequence, no moment is as vital as the ever-so-brief moment in which the Entry occurs. If we look at our velocity curve, we see a rapid deceleration of the speed of the shell just before the Entry. This deceleration can be far steeper than any acceleration during the Drive and continues past the point of immersion of the blades. Your actions here have an enormous impact on the speed of the boat. Putting your weight on the foot stretcher at any time before the blade is loaded seriously increases this deceleration. Of all the technical aspects of the stroke, this is the one which will probably take the most time. The good news is that it does not have to be perfect NOW. Any small improvement will improve your speed tremendously.

■ Squaring the Blades ■

Wind and water conditions dictate when you should square your blades. The only important things are that the hands are soft at the Entry allowing even under-squared blades to be corrected by the water and that the blades not be rowed in on the Drive.

If you are rowing into a head wind, keep your blades feathered for as long as is necessary to still be able to make a clean Entry. If there is a following wind and the water is not so rough as to make the Recovery difficult, square your blades rather early and let them serve as sails. The important thing is to be comfortable and get a clean Entry; exactly when you square the blades is not critical. (See Hand Hold and Feathering)

■ Geometry and Physics ■

Now it is necessary for a brief conversation about the geometry and physics of the stroke. First the geometry. When the blades enter the water, there is a brief moment, ever so brief yet so significant, when they are actually moving against the "stream" or flow of the water along the hull toward what, were you in a race, would be called the "finish line." The whole system—you, oars and boat—are all moving in this direction before the tip of the blade begins to arc toward the "starting line" or stern of the boat.

Now, the physics. The blade of an oar has a convex surface on the bow-facing side and a concave surface on the stern-facing side.

Bernoulli's Principle tells us that the faster a fluid travels over a surface, the less the pressure on that surface. Since the water is passing faster over the convex surfaces of the blades than over their concave surfaces, there is less pressure on the convex surfaces and more pressure on the concave surfaces. This pressure differential is what is called "lift" and is, of course, how airplanes fly. So, in the same way that an airfoil or a wing acts to create lift, our blades create lift as they enter the water.

Therefore, since lift is always perpendicular to the flow of the fluid over the surface, the direction of the lift force that is created when the blades enter the water is somewhat towards the bow. The blades will actually be pulled in that direction. Your signal that this is happening is when you feel the handles of your oars pull gently into your fingers towards the stern, pulled, as it were, by Daniel Bernoulli.

In rowing, all this is somewhat controversial. This propulsive force, which is the result of the interaction of the forces of lift (which are always perpendicular to the flow of the fluid) and drag (which are always parallel to the flow of the fluid) on the blade, may or may not be enough to actually pull the boat. But that is not what seems to me to be the most important aspect of these forces. It is certainly enough to pull the blade—if we let it.

Furthermore, this phenomenon will only take place if your hands are relaxed and soft and you are not driving the blade into the water with your legs (or your back). Any attempt to apply "instantaneous" pressure against the foot stretcher as the blades touch the water and to spring "simultaneously" into the Drive (as we have so often heard) will work against the geometry and the physics of this phenomenon. And it will be disastrous to the run of the boat.

The period of time between when the blade drops into the water and begins to get pulled by Bernoulli towards the bow and when the blade reverses direction and begins to arc around toward the stern is very brief, about as long as the snap of one's fingers. To the rower, however, it should feel like "Dead Time" (something almost unthinkable under all our past models of "the catch"). However, it is not wasted time. We need to occupy this time by holding our pressure against the pins (connected through our core/elbows), which will allow the water to firmly grab our blades and hence pull the blades toward the bow and the handles toward the stern. Of course, this requires enormous patience, relaxed legs, soft hands and Stability. We must allow the blades to do what they want to do, nothing more or less. **In other words, we must simply stay out of the way!**

■ Swimming Analogy ■

The effect of Bernoulli's Principle on one's blades during this "dead time" is the same as the effect of water on one's hands during a swimming stroke. For example, if we look at the crawl stroke, the hand slices into the water trying for as little turbulence as possible. This hand entry is made short of full arm extension. The swimmer's arm then extends out to full reach under the water, moving against the stream or flow of the oncoming water. The swimmer's hand thus acts as a foil; because the faster movement of the water over the back of the hand compared to its slower movement along the palm creates a pressure differential, we get lift.

This is the same force that is at work on your blades. Just as our swimmer thrusts his hands forward against the oncoming flow of water, you can think of achieving your full stroke length when you continue—even after your blades are already in the water—to separate your handles, ever so slightly, and to push your blades gently against the stream just as the blades are being sucked forward by Bernoulli. What you are doing is allowing and assisting the blades to do what they want to do. This is the difference between working with the water rather than against it.

The application of light pressure against the flow of the water seems counter-intuitive to an oarsman, who naturally assumes that this would stop the boat. However, it is not counter-intuitive to a fish. Think of a fish swimming upstream by the gentle undulation of its body as it applies pressure against the flow of the water. It is being pulled upstream and without this undulation, our little fish would go tail-first over the waterfall.

Whether these same perpendicular lift forces on a rower's blades are enough to actually pull the rower and the boat forward and to therefore increase the boat's speed would be very difficult to measure. However, what is important is that this, along with the parallel drag forces, is what holds your blades secure in the water as you prepare to initiate the Drive. For it is in this brief period of dead time after the Entry and before your blades begin to swing toward the stern that your blades are "locking-on" to the water.

You must allow this to happen by not being too violent or dramatic at the Entry. As the blades are being pulled, go with them, while keeping your core engaged and working into the blade. And go with them lightly. Again, let the blades do what they want to do.

What happens to the wrist of the swimmer during the arm stroke is both fascinating and complicated. For example, let us say that at the entry, as the swimmer's arm extends, the angle of his upper arm and armpit is 120 degrees while the angle of his upper arm and forearm is 180 degrees. The wrist might be 10 degrees out and back. When his arm begins to bend, as the armpit angle closes and the upper arm/forearm angle diminishes, his wrist rotates and changes pitch, down and back. These numerous small changes in his wrists' pitch throughout the stroke are the swimmer's subconscious responses to the forces of lift and drag. One could never coach these subtle changes. They depend upon "soft" hands and wrists—and minimal turbulence—in short, a feel for the water. Those who have this capacity are the faster swimmers. The same thing is true for rowers.

How these forces of lift and drag are affected by the changing pitch of the blade as it moves through the water would be an interesting topic of research. This, in turn, would involve the question of what is the optimal pitch on the pin, both lateral pitch and fore/aft pitch. Or is no pitch at all better? Or does it even matter? Certainly, there is a good deal of variation in the pitch and angles of the wrists of very successful swimmers. For rowers, other factors are probably of more importance, such as allowing the blades to be locked on while you are stable and off your feet.

Suggested Drills:

- Skimming (#4)
- Newtons (#7)
- Front End (#10)

Summary of the Recovery—from Release to Entry

Everything begins with the Release. Make yourself that Fortress of Stability.

A boat on water, like the water itself, will follow the path of least resistance. Allow it to float; stay out of its way. That means you must make a commitment to keeping your blades off the water. Blades hitting the water during the Recovery, though psychologically reassuring, do not aid stability; they hinder it, removing you from your connection to the boat, and putting your attention on your hands.

Any effort on your part to "control" the shell during the Recovery is going to constrain it from taking the path it wants to take. Let it rock; let it roll; let it bob; let it weave. Make yourself stable relative to the shell, not the water. Not since New Testament times has it been possible to be stable relative to water!

Distribute your weight throughout the shell by transferring it onto the riggers in a stable manner. Keep from centralizing your weight either on the seat or the feet because this will only interfere with the run of the boat (i.e., don't try to "balance" the shell).

Obviously, you cannot physically leave the seat or the foot stretchers; but you can "un-weight" yourself from them. You do this through supporting your weight on the riggers and pins by engaging your core through your elbows as though you were supporting your frame on a jungle gym and allowing your hips and legs to "swing" freely. Your belly and chest muscles lift up and connect you to the pins through your elbows while the major muscles of your back draw your weight onto the riggers by pushing down and against the pins. Ski the moguls. Keep your hips and legs as relaxed as possible and avoid using your legs to pull yourself into the stern. Think of being on a skateboard and drawing yourself through a doorway by spreading your arms and elbows out and back.

Keep the Recovery 100% upper body and ride the riggers into and BEYOND the Entry. In other words, don't just stay off the foot stretchers for 15/16ths of the Recovery—stay off for 17/16ths of it!

The Drive

Chapter **4**

Once the blade has entered the water and been accepted and Bernoulli has grabbed and pulled, the blade then begins to arc around toward the stern. This is caused by the forward movement of the shell and causes the handles to come back toward you. You do not have to be the agent of this transition!

After this brief "Dead Time", while you are softly "undulating" and allowing the blades to "fill up" or get loaded, the feeling of pressure seems to switch to the face of the blade. Another way of looking at this is to think of letting the water "load your feet" before you press sharply against the foot stretcher. Once this has happened—you are now in familiar territory.

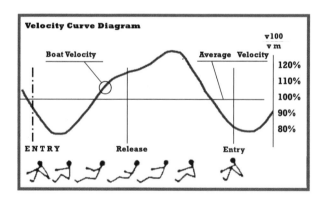

Pressure on the foot stretcher **before** the blade gets **"loaded"** checks the speed of the boat. **Wait** for the water to **"load the feet"** before **driving.**

Applying pressure on the inside of the foot, drive off the pad of your big toe against the foot stretcher and suspend your weight over the handles and your hips (and against the pins). As Edmond Ware, who is often referred to as the "Father of British Orthodox Rowing," wrote in the early 1900's, "A man in rowing should economize his strength by the right use of his weight. His weight is always with him in the boat. If he is rowing badly his strength will soon evaporate"—(Grammar of Rowing).

Of course, do not actually leave your seat. If you have downhill skiing experience, you will recognize this feeling of "unweighting" your feet through turns without your skis actually leaving the snow.

If your Entry has been soft, the blades will set at the correct depth. (See Rigging and Center of Gravity). As soon as you have begun to press against the foot stretcher with the inside of your foot (ball joint of the big toe), push your heels down onto the base of the footplate. Even if you have sufficient flexibility in your ankles to have them remain on the footplate during the Recovery, begin the Drive off the big toe and then shift to the whole foot. Do not gradually roll your feet down during the Drive. Snap them down! Getting them down quickly stabilizes the boat. It also gives you a solid platform from which to suspend your weight. Finally, it signals when you can begin to open your back—which is as soon as your heels are down.

Suspend yourself on the "oars", **over** your **hips**. Use your **weight** to move the shell. This is similar to **suspending yourself** on a rope.

Driving off the inside of the foot aligns your ankles with your knees and makes for a more direct power application without your knees "wobbling" on the first part of the Drive. Driving off the ball of your foot engages the smaller, quicker calf and quadricep muscles so that you have a sharper beginning of the Drive.

Quickly pushing the heels down and driving through them engages your powerful, major leg muscles, the gluteus maximi and hamstrings. Gradually rolling the heels down, staying on your toes too long, actually forces you to push your weight into the bottom of the boat as you move through the Drive, and causes you to rely mostly upon your quadriceps and calf muscles for your leg power.

At this point, as always, you should be pushing the button against the pin towards the blade. Keep the same awareness of your relationship to the pin as you had on the Recovery. Keep a "sparrow hold" on the handles. (See Hand Hold/Feathering). Power is generated from your major muscles while suspending your body weight. No power is generated from the hands! Do not be concerned with bringing the handles towards you. They will do that on their own. Do not try to turn your shell into an ergometer. You have the same vectors on the Drive that you had on the Recovery, always into the pin, toward the blade. Again, imagine that you have your eyeballs on your elbows and that they are always looking at your blades. This image will be particularly useful when moving into the final stage of the arm draw into the Release.

The Power Clean Weight Lift is my model for the Drive. This lift begins with pressure against the floor (your foot plate in a shell). Once the hips have engaged and the bar has come up off the floor, the bar is aggressively accelerated by a powerful thrust of the hips "into the bar" as it begins to come above the knees. This "middle third" is the main thrust of the power clean lift and the rowing Drive. The main difference between the lift and your Drive is that the Drive is more explosive after the momentary "Dead Time".

It is extremely interesting to observe how the arms operate during this lift. As the bar is being explosively accelerated the elbows move outward as the arms begin to break. The bar rises to around your sternum and then you drop under the bar and "catch" it. While the lats and trapezius muscles stay engaged, there is very little movement of the upper arms, very little "pull" through the upper arms. The elbows move more out than up. This is quite similar to what you want to do during the Drive.

Once you have become the active agent (the male principle), i.e. after the handles have begun to come toward you and you are driving the legs and suspending your weight, it is important to hold a firm core all the way to the Release by contracting the muscles of your abdomen and holding your navel into your spine.

While constantly driving your knees away from your body (not prying your body away from your knees), the handles should travel in a path from the point of the Entry, following your center of gravity, to a point somewhere just below the lower tip of your sternum at the back end of the Drive (Release). This path will be a very slight arc because your center of gravity is lower relative to the water/boat at the Entry, rises slightly as you "open your back" and then lowers again relative to the water as you complete your layback. If your rigging is correct and your Entry soft, you should not have to exert any effort to hold the handles at your center of gravity and the blades at their proper depth.

The back begins to open when the heels are firmly planted on the foot stretcher. Although this is, in fact, much closer to the very beginning of the Drive than the "middle third', you can think of it as the commencement of

As your **center of gravity** rises and then lowers relative to the shell (and water), the handles should **follow this path** and our imaginary oars must necessarily go **slightly deeper** and **then shallower** in the water during the **Drive**.

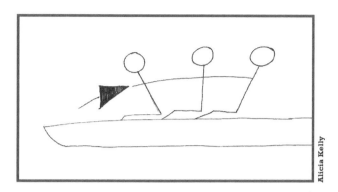

Alicia Kelly

this middle third. For this middle third is biomechanically the point in the Drive of maximum power. That maximum power is generated by the legs and the body swing. Again, it is important not to yank the handles. **Do not try to turn your boat into an ergometer**. Continue to work against the pins.

As you pass through the middle third of the Drive, your upper body begins to gain strength relative to your legs, which start to lose biomechanical advantage as they approach becoming straight. (Think of trying to do a leg press beginning with your legs nearly straight. You have very little power and will not be able to move the weight.) As you begin to feel your body weight settle onto the seat (but before it actually HAS settled)— which will be somewhere toward the end of the middle third of the Drive—begin the arm draw. However, even as your elbows begin to break, continue to suspend your weight on the pins, thereby maintaining the feeling of being "unweighted" from the seat. Indeed, the drawing of your arms should continue your suspension all the way up to the point of releasing the blades from the water.

The point and manner at which you begin the arm draw, joining the legs and back, are extremely important. Everyone will have a slightly different point at which to do this. This is an issue of Feel. However, wherever you start it, it should never be jerky. In fact, if the front end of your Drive (Entry and the beginning of the Drive) has been effective and if the middle third has been powerful, your arms will not be able to add anything. Instead, they will just be able to hang on and continue the suspension of your body until all three components thereof, the legs, the back and arms, have completed the Drive at as close to the same time as is possible.

The Drive

Again, looking at a velocity curve of a single stroke, we see that the speed of the shell begins to level off during the last part of the Drive. Any effort to increase the speed at this time (sometimes referred to as "accelerating into the finish") will be a serious waste of energy. You simply cannot accelerate the boat, i.e., speed it up, at this point. All you will do is stop working with the water and begin to rip your blades through the water, thereby, slowing the boat, losing stability and messing up the proper release point.

Once again, this is a question of FEEL—feel of pressure against the pin, feel of the foot stretcher, feel of the water on the blade and feel of the general movement of the boat. If you are focusing upon your suspension and applying constant pressure against the pin in the direction of the blade, FEEL for these things will become second nature to you. And you thought the Drive was all about POWER.

During the last part of the Drive, as your elbows angle out from your sides, staying in front of your belly and continuing to push into the pins ("looking at" the blades with the eyes you have put on them), they will seem to be changing direction. As this happens, make sure your shoulders are rolled forward thereby keeping your shoulder girdle stable. Feel as though you are drawing your back through your shoulders and into your elbows in the direction of the pins. Do this without "bucking or lugging" into that position of intense stability which we call the Fortress of Stability. There should be very little movement of the upper arms and they should definitely not be pulling into the bow. (See Release/Follow-Through and Hulk Illustration)

As mentioned, the legs, back and arms should finish at as close to the same time as is possible. Just as the backs of your legs hit the seat deck, while your blades are still "loaded", push your blades out of the water. Do not pull your oars out of the water with your hands or arms! Push them out with your feet. Remember, there is no added on "finish", no aggressive yank of the oar handles; it is Drive–Release, Drive–Release. **There is no finish. Just let it go!**

Suggested Drills:

■ Feet Out (#10)
■ Radical Finishectomy (#18)

Summary of the Drive—never Pull, always Draw

The Drive begins after the entry of the blade into the water by pushing on the foot stretcher with the inside of the foot off the pad of the big toe. As soon as you have done this, get your heels down and suspend your weight, "unweight", by Drawing your weight onto the handles and riggers. Do not think of pulling the handles! Keeping your weight over your hips, and drawing yourself onto the handles and riggers as you push off the foot stretcher, drive your knees away from your body, pushing into the pins. Do not pull the handles. A shell is not an ergometer. Our model for the drive is the Power Clean. The push of the legs and the thrust of the hips as the back opens accelerates the shell, and hence the oar handles.

As the handles come toward you, the arms will naturally bend. Continue keeping your weight above the handles by pushing with the legs AND DRAWING through your core onto the handles/riggers/pins until the backs of your knees hit the seat deck. Keeping your elbows in front of your body (there is no Finish) mantle out of the water.

Remember to always hold your navel drawn into your spine and to keep your shoulders in that forward Hulk position, never out of their sockets or hunched.

■ A Note on Layback ■

The amount of layback people get seems to change from year to year, depending on who won the World Championships. Nonetheless, there are several basic principles which need to be adhered to, no matter whether you are a man or a woman, young or old.

First, the amount of layback you get has a direct impact on the angle of your oars at the Release. Too much layback and your blades will come in too close to the hull of your shell and lose the vortex or "hollow" which has followed them into the stern during the Drive. Water will fill this hollow in and come crashing into your blades. This will force you to wrestle them out of the water. If you are coming to sculling through a sweep background (or your coach has, and many sculling coaches have), you will not be likely to be paying attention to this issue. In a sweep boat, because your body gets in the way of the oar handle, you virtually cannot lose the hollow. You will probably lose a kidney before you lose the vortex. However, in a sculling boat, it is easy to get too much layback into the bow, pulling the handles too far into the bow and, thus, losing the vortex.

Secondly, too much layback drives the bow of the shell deeper into the water, creating more resistance on the hull and slowing the boat down. You can easily detect that this is happening if you see your shell throwing up an increased bow wave.

In addition, through excessive layback, not only will you have driven the hull deeper into the water during the layback itself, you will then, as Sir Isaac Newton tells us in his third law of motion ("for every action there is an equal and opposite reaction"), give the shell a secondary "bounce-back" into the water as you begin to sit back up. Not a good thing!

Finally, you can compromise your core/frame stability. For example, let's say you can sit at your computer for several hours comfortably with 6 degrees of layback. If you go even to 8 degrees, you might feel a tightening or tensing of the muscles in your lower back. The way you will relieve this without even thinking about it will be to release your lower back and slump or collapse. The amount of layback that one can comfortably tolerate will vary from one person to the next, depending on body types. While you might be comfortable at 6 degrees, someone else might be comfortable up to and even beyond 10 degrees. Accordingly, layback is idiosyncratic. Nevertheless, everyone has his/her limits and once you pass out of your comfort zone, you jeopardize your stability. **And, as we know, if you are not stable, you are not able**.

Suggested Drills:

- Front End (#8)
- Blending the Drive (#9)
- Feet Out(#10)
- Radical Finishectomy (#18)

Breathing

Chapter **5**

Obviously, breathing is extremely important for supplying oxygen to your muscles and for the removal of CO_2 from your lungs. It is also very important in establishing and sustaining your rhythm and stability. Yet, this is an element of the stroke which is often overlooked.

You need to establish a breathing pattern that will meet all your needs from practice to racing, paddling to sprinting, and short courses to head racing, so that you will not be forced to change your pattern to fit your circumstances.

Your Basic Pattern should be to inhale at the Entry, hold your breath during the Drive and exhale forcefully at the Release. The inhale takes place naturally as you respond to your muscles' demands for oxygen. In fact, you generally take in considerably more oxygen than you actually need. It is the exhale, however, which requires particular attention. This is because your lungs actually fill up with CO_2 and you have no internal mechanism which tells you to get rid of the CO_2. This build-up of CO_2 can cause the sensation of being "short of breath" because there is less and less room in your lungs for fresh oxygen. Furthermore, the exchange of oxygen into the bloodstream is much more efficient in the lower regions of your lungs. Therefore, you should take care to exhale as much CO_2 from your lungs as possible.

Under stressful conditions, e.g., racing, you will need two exhales per stroke to get rid of this build up. So, in addition to your Basic Pattern of inhaling at the Entry and exhaling at the Release, you should add another exhale. Two exhales are the key. Now, since you cannot exhale twice without inhaling a second time in between, you must add a secondary, minor, inhale during the Recovery.

This can seem somewhat complicated. However, don't be thinking: inhale at the Entry, hold the breath during the Drive, exhale at the Release, inhale after the body rock, and exhale just before inhaling at the next Entry. It is much easier to simply think of the Basic Pattern and then, after the body rock, simply do not hold your breath during the Recovery, and make sure your exhales are forceful.

After a short period of practice (see Erging), this will result in a very natural rhythm of breathing with two forceful exhales that take care of all your needs.

Some physicians will tell you that it is dangerous to hold your breath during the Drive. And while we have the example of weight lifters who are taught to exhale during the power phase of their lift, it is safe for rowers to hold their breath during the power phase. This is because no individual stroke approaches the type of extreme or maximum exertion that we see from power lifters.

One of the potentially unfortunate consequences of exhaling at the Release is that the process of exhaling, i.e., the depression of the diaphragm which compresses the lungs and therefore forces the built-up CO_2 up and out, also tends to make one collapse the upper body at the Release. This is, of course, the very time when you want to be a Fortress of Stability.

However, there is a nice pilates/yoga exercise which corrects this. Rather than thinking about your diaphragm depressing, think of following the breath. As the diaphragm depresses, expand your rib cage. The CO_2 passes up and out. Imagine a bellows: one end squeezes and the other expands. Following the breath up and out and expanding the chest helps you to sit up and keep your necessary vertical orientation, rather collapsing like a balloon.

Rhythm

Chapter **6**

If your Release has been executed at the correct time, i.e., just as the backs of your legs have hit the seat deck, your blades will have sprung out of the water and changed direction almost effortlessly, bringing you seamlessly into the Recovery. On the other hand, if you have been accustomed to making the Release too late, i.e., your stroke is too long at the back end, you will have wrestled your blades out of the water in a disruptive, jerky manner. The tendency will be to "stop at the finish" and rest at this point with no Follow-Through. This rest interrupts the release of energy which has been stored in the oars during the Drive. Among other things, it is this utilization of the energy of the Drive which creates a sense of Flow, this wonderful feeling of ease and rhythm that you are after.

By the way, "Finish" is another word, along with "balance" and "catch", which might help improve your rowing if you eliminated it, or entered it into the Lexicon of Bad Rowing. The words we use to describe things have a huge impact on how we think about those things. Just as "catch" gives you the impression that there is something which you can, in fact, catch, "finish" gives you the notion that something has "finished". Given that idea, many people stop at the Release, and only then begin the Recovery.

You do not want to rest at the Release. This not only breaks the rhythm of the stroke and wastes the stored energy which the oars build up during the Drive, but it also forces you to waste your own energy in order to begin the stroke cycle all over again. After the Release and Follow–Through and the subsequent rotation of your pelvis as you swing your body forward over your knees, you have an opportunity to rest. However, resting does not mean becoming a bean bag! Think of it more as enjoying a period of "firm relaxation".

Many coaches speak of the importance of "ratio" during the Recovery. What they are really after is this sense of flow. If a boat is moving with this sense of flow, the perception is that the Recovery is taking twice or even three times as long as the Drive— while the reality is that, at least when racing at full speed, the ratio of Recovery to Drive is much closer to one to one.

This feeling of flow, of rhythm, begins with an effortless extraction of the blade from the water and continues with a seamless change of direction of the oar handle, all the while keeping continuous pressure against the pins, and maintaining a firm connection of one's core/frame to the frame of the boat.

As mentioned, breathing is another important element in establishing rhythm. In general, it centers you in your boat and allows you to establish a consistent cycle of repetitive movements. Moreover, on the Recovery, it aids you in making a seamless transition from the Release to the Recovery and, eventually, to the Entry.

As you complete the Release, your hands should swing away naturally, following the speed of the boat. Once this is accomplished and your body has swung over, you must relax your hips and legs and resist the temptation to "pull" yourself up the slide. You should feel as though your seat and your handles are traveling at the same speed of the boat. This will give you a sense that the stroke is coming to you, not that you are going to it. This creates the rhythm that we strive for, the feeling of stillness as you flow into the Entry, moving with the speed of the boat.

Essential Rigging

Chapter **7**

Rigging is a subject dealt with in a number of good books. Consequently, it is not my intention here to go into many of the details of rigging. It can be a complicated subject which deserves its own study. However, if you do look through the available studies, there are a couple things which you should keep in mind.

First, most of the figures and numbers listed for settings are not necessarily appropriate for scullers other than the population from which they were collected, which is generally elite rowers. In other words, it is not valid to extrapolate, as many of these books suggest you do, from what oarlock span, oar length, oar inboard, etc. are being used by elite level rowers if you are a recreational rower or a Masters rower, even if you row competitively. My general impression is that most scullers who are not in the elite category row with a "load" (or the ratio of inboard to outboard within the context of the span, or measured distance from pin to pin, while also considering the blade size and even stiffness of the shaft) which is too heavy.

Secondly, when considering what load is right for you, sometimes you have to forget all the numbers and rig the boat so that it fits you comfortably. For example, you want to have your hands in a comfortable position at the Release such that you are stable and your blades are at the optimal position at the Release and then again at the Entry. This means, among other things, that, depending upon your size, you may have to have much shorter oars and a shorter span than you will ever see in these books.

The three basic rigging considerations are: Oarlock Height, Foot Stretcher Placement and Span.

Oarlock Height. It is absolutely essential for the proper application of power and your ability to suspend your weight while keeping your blades at the proper depth that your oarlocks are set at the right height. When the blades are buried at the Entry with little or no shaft in the water, your oar handles should be at your Center of Gravity, i.e., the point at which half of your body's mass is above and half of it is below an imaginary dividing line. Rowing with your handles following this imaginary line is a function of the height of your oarlocks.

If your oarlocks are set too high, your handles will be too high when the blade is buried. As a result, you will struggle with your shoulders to hold on to this proper depth. Your handles will seek out your center of gravity and begin a downward path. Just as you are probably not strong enough to hold the handles above your center of gravity at the Entry, you will not be able to stop this downward path of the handles during the Drive and they will pass right through your center of gravity into your lap at the back end of the Drive, causing you to "wash out". Indeed, if you are rowing hard, it will be even more difficult for you to keep your blades buried throughout the Drive.

On the other hand, if your oarlocks are set too low, your handles will be below your center of gravity at the Entry and you will have to bring your handles up to your center of gravity during the stroke for efficient power application. This will force your blades too deep and you will struggle to get them out cleanly.

An easy way to find your Center of Gravity is to imagine that you are in a one-on-one rope pull, or "tug of war". Stand with your feet planted shoulder width apart with one in front of the other and imagine that you are taking hold of the rope, exactly where you want it. Most likely you have found your center of gravity. Half your mass will be above this point and half will be below it. It is the point where you will best be able to use your body weight by simply leaning back. This is the same path that your oar handles should follow during the Drive in order for you to maximize the force that you can generate by doing nothing more than making use of the weight of your own body.

Foot Stretcher Placement. This has everything to do with the proper point at which you execute the Release, which, in turn, affects your ability to get your blades out of the water cleanly.

If you extend a line through the pins out perpendicular to your boat, the optimal angle formed by your oar at the Release will vary roughly somewhere between 35 and 40 degrees. The exact point that you should be looking for is that point at the back end of the Drive where the hollow, or small vortex, which forms in the water off the back of your blade during the Drive is still there when you execute your Release. If you have set your feet too far into the bow, the oar angle will be too severe and your blades will have swung too far in toward the hull, thereby allowing each vortex to spin off the back side of its blade before the blade is extracted from the water. When this happens, water quickly fills this hole in and slaps into the back of the blade, thus causing you to get "stuck" and to feel as though you are "wrestling" your blades out of the water. This not only has a tremendously adverse impact upon the speed of your shell, but it also wastes a large amount of energy.

The Release should feel as effortless as the Entry. When made at the correct point, the blades will jump out of the water, releasing the energy of the Drive, which is stored in the shafts. This energy is used to help in the transition from the Drive into the Release and Follow-Through. Most scullers are too long at the Release. Foot stretcher placement has everything to do with this. (See Radical Finishectomy drill #18)

When your legs are flat and you are sitting at the back end of the Drive in a comfortable layback position, you ideally want your handles to be a fist-width apart when they are a thumb's-distance from your body. I call this ideal the Rule of Thumbs. However, it is an ideal which is not often achieved. Body types being different, not everyone can make this happen without a great deal of experimenting with such things as span and oar length, etc. This "tweaking" may be neither practical nor productive. The important factor is that the handles are close enough to your body so that you are in a strong and stable—and comfortable—position which allows you to mantle out of the water.

At the Florida Rowing Center, the first thing we do when getting scullers into their boats is to set their foot stretchers at the place where they can comply with the Rule of Thumbs. This is because we want them to be comfortable at the Release. Then, while they are rowing, we look at where this places their blade at the Release. Is the hollow still behind their blade when it exits the water? Because most scullers are too long at the Release, we find that we usually have to move people further and further into the stern from their initial setting in order to optimize their Release point.

Another important consideration for foot stretcher placement is facilitating length at the Entry. Length at the Entry is extremely important. However, it needs to be effective length, not maximal length.

Try to set your foot stretchers such that the "swivel" point of your hips ends up about as far sternward of or "through" the pins at the Entry as your boat will allow without your shins coming quite to the perpendicular. It used to be considered that perpendicular shins were optimal; however, I think this is actually quite a bit past optimal. You only need to sit in a leg press machine with "perpendicular shins", i.e., with your knees over your ankles, and see how much weight you can press compared to what you can do with a little less angle. It is significant! Furthermore, since we get our length from handle separation rather than from squeaking out a bit more leg compression, you don't need to get your legs into what is a biomechanically compromised position in order to optimize your length.

Within reason, the further you can rig your boat "through the pins", without being so far into the stern so as to cause your boat to "porpoise" or dip down in the stern, the better. This allows you to get more length at the Entry—and less at the Release, where you may be in danger of losing your vortex if you are too long. Although there is a point when one is rigged too far through the pins and the load on the blade at the Entry becomes too uncomfortable to tolerate, it is unlikely that you will be able to rig yourself that far into the stern of your shell. If you do, simply move your foot stretchers back slightly (or give yourself a bit more Span–see below).

One of the many great things about wing riggers is that they often have several settings which allow you to move the rigger fore and aft if you need to get further through the pin at the Entry or further away from your handles at the Release. This means that once you have established your proper position with regard to the trim of the shell (not so far into the bow as to force it down at the Release nor so far into the stern as to cause it to dive at the Entry), you can change how close or far away you are from the pins and handles by moving the riggers without upsetting the trim of the boat as it moves through the water.

Span. This is the distance measured from the center of one pin to the center of the other. Basically, the width of the span governs the length of the stroke when the blades are in the water. The greater the span, the shorter the length in the water and the shorter the span, the greater the length in the water. This, however, is quite hypothetical because many scullers lack the flexibility to take advantage of the potential length of the stroke which is theoretically allowed by their span.

For many scullers, rather than approaching span from a "load" perspective (the greater the length of the stroke, or time the blades are in the water, the greater the "load"), it is equally important to factor in comfort and biomechanics. For example, if you have short legs and try to adjust through the pins, you may not be able to come close to complying with the Rule of Thumbs;

instead you may find that when you are sitting with your legs flat at the Release, the handles of your oars are pushed right into your stomach. Moving the foot stretchers further into the bow will only make matters worse at the Entry because no matter what the span numbers indicate, you will be so far behind the pins that getting any reasonable length at the Entry will be impossible. In addition, if you shorten the span in order to increase your length in the water, you may well have so much "overlap" of the oar handles as they swing away as to make the Follow-Through difficult and uncomfortable. Indeed, in the mid to last part of the Drive, things will likely be downright awkward.

For comfort and proper mechanics, a general rule is to have between 5 to 9 centimeters of oar handle overlap when the oars are perpendicular to the boat. This means that if you divide the span by 2 (getting the distance from the center of the boat to the center of one pin) your inboard (the distance from the end of the handle to the Blade-side face of the button) should be between 5 to 9 centimeters greater than that number. For example, for a span of 160 cm, your buttons should be set so that you have an inboard of between 85 and 89 cm. At the Florida Rowing Center, where we use hatchet oars of 285 centimeters in length, we begin by setting our rigging at 160 centimeters span and 85 centimeters inboard.

Hand Hold and Feathering

Chapter **8**

It is probably no exaggeration to say that perhaps 90% of scullers have been told by their coaches not to use their wrists to feather their blades! However, it is probably also not an exaggeration to say that at least 85% of scullers do this, many going so far as to use their wrists to "feather their blades out of the water". Indeed, even many "elite" scullers feather their blades out with their wrists. So, how bad can it be?

Thinking back to our maxim of making you into a piece of the equipment and transferring your core strength into the riggers/pins through your elbows, you can see that a bend in your wrists at the Release is not a very good connection. You certainly would never design a piece of equipment with a bend like that in it. Furthermore, bending your wrists at the Release focuses your attention on your hands and away from your core/frame. So, learn to feather without your wrists!

Feathering can be difficult and depends upon the correct hand-hold. As far as I can tell, every movement you make during the rowing stroke is replicated in the "real world"—except feathering! It involves many muscles in your hand which run up your forearm and which you simply never use in the manner necessary to feather a blade.

To practice feathering, you do not need an oar, a dowel or a salt shaker (contrary to what numerous coaches suggest). Just hold your hands up in front of you with the palms away. Keep your wrists flat and count your knuckles from the tips of your fingers down. You have first knuckles, second knuckles and then a set of large third knuckles. Now, while still keeping your wrists flat, curl your fingers down from the first (smallest) and the second knuckles, keeping the space between the second and third knuckles flat. To practice feathering your imaginary blade, while keeping those fingers tightly curled, raise the second knuckles and depress the third. Finally, to square your "oar", simply reverse things by lowering the second knuckles.

For the purpose of practice, it is absolutely essential to keep the fingers tightly curled. This isolates the movement of the fingers around the axis of the third knuckles. Practice this for considerable time before trying it with an oar.

Note that the thumb is not involved in this process. In fact, to feather without breaking your wrist downward, it is helpful to release the thumb from the face of the handle. If the thumb "pushes forward", as many suggest, it will necessarily pull the wrist downward. Furthermore, the thumb remaining on the face of the handle hinders the handle from rotating (which it obviously must do in order to move the blade from being on the square to being on the feather).

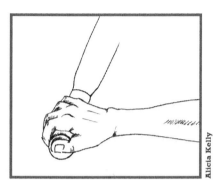

Large knuckles of the **index** and **middle finger** are on the **crest** of the handle when the blade is squared.

In order to feather and square with a real oar, you must have a proper hand-hold. Now, let us consider the hand-hold itself. First of all, it is important not to squeeze the juice out of the handle. You want to hold the handle as though you were holding a sparrow. Softly use the bones of the fingers to protect the bird without letting it fly away. Remember, your main connection to the pins comes through your elbows, not your hands. The hands must remain soft. (Note that this is why we don't call the hand-hold the "grip". "Grip" is another word, along with "catch", "finish" and "balance", which is best dispatched to the Lexicon of Bad Rowing.)

The location of your hand on the oar is a critical feature of the hand-hold and its impact upon your ability to properly feather and square the blade. When the blade is squared in the water, extend your arms and keep your wrists flat. Place your hand on top of the handle with the third knuckles on the crest of the oar's curvature. Actually, it is the third knuckles of the middle and index fingers which are key; or more precisely, the pads of the hand underneath the knuckles of the middle and index fingers. When you depress the third knuckles and raise the second, it is the pads which are in contact with the oar handle on its crest, working with the section of your fingers between the second and first knuckles as they rise up, which roll the blade onto the feather. If, however, your handle is too far into your palm—and even a little is too much—when you depress your third knuckles and raise the second, your wrist is going to have to break. On the other hand, if your handle is "in the fingers", you will have no control of the handle and, again, you will be forced to break your wrist to feather the blade.

$\mathbf{A}$s previously stated, the thumb is not involved in feathering or squaring the oar and should be released from the end/face of the handle if the oar is to rotate smoothly without using the wrist. The only function your thumb plays in the hand-hold is to let you know where the end of the handle is. The thumb only applies sufficient pressure to prevent your hand from sliding down the handle; it should not be involved in applying pressure against the pins.

Learning to feather properly takes a great deal of practice, but to many rowers, it hardly seems worth it. If you are one of these slugs, keep in mind that the most important thing about the Release is to make sure that it is made by mantling, hinging the forearm at the elbow from your core and extracting the blade when it is square. Feathering the blade out of the water is completely unacceptable! So, don't be a slug; do the necessary hard work and learn to feather properly.

Backing

Chapter 9

When learning to scull, the first skill you should master is how to back. It is the most important skill to have for general safety and also will give you tremendous confidence. It is also relatively easy to learn.

As a novice rower (or an experienced one, for that matter), you will find yourself in many situations where it is essential to be able to back your boat away from trouble. If the only way you know how to manipulate your shell is by pulling (rowing with) one oar or the other, you will not be able to extricate yourself from these situations and end up drawing the boat further into trouble. Backing is an absolutely essential skill!

I don't believe that it is necessary to turn your blades upside down. You are not looking for maximum efficiency. You are looking, often, for the quickest way out of a situation, a situation which may require you to back one moment and then row the next with little or no time to be turning your blades upside down and then flipping them right side up.

Reverse Feather. The **top tip** of the blade is rotated toward the **stern** of the shell.

Practice, at first, in an area large enough so that you can maneuver your shell first one way, then the other. Practice with one oar backing for a few strokes and then use the other. While pushing the handle away from yourself, try to keep the other oar blade resting flat on the surface of the water with your hands at as close to the same plane as possible without them colliding with each other as you back one away. Keeping the handles on as close to the same plane as possible keeps the boat level and makes extracting the blade and returning the handle to your body easier. When first learning, it is not necessary to "feather" the blade; simply push the handles down enough to clear the water on the return. After you become comfortable with this, you can "reverse feather" the blades by rolling the hand forward.

While backing, you do not want to come too far up the slide into the stern. Keep your strokes short and use very little or no slide. After you have mastered using one oar at a time, try using two together and then progress to alternating one, then the other, with one oar backing while the other is returning to your body. Finally learn a "River Turn" whereby you push one handle away while drawing the other (rowing) toward you.

Competitive Rowing

Racing Starts

Chapter **10**

Some scullers do not do anything differently for the start of a race from what they do for a regular training piece. They simply begin rowing hard and go from there. Others have a specific routine and set number of strokes, often rowed at a higher and shorter length than the others and either gradually "settle" into their race cadence as they lengthen out or they "settle" in a set number of strokes. Regardless of your tactic, the most important thing about starts is getting off the line cleanly. Do not try to cover the entire course in the first five strokes.

I suggest a basic five stroke sequence for racing starts. Each stroke has a specific purpose.

First Stroke: this is different from every other stroke you take. Its purpose is simply to overcome inertia and get the boat moving away as cleanly as possible. While some prefer beginning at 1/2 slide, I like 3/4 slide. The only real difference is one of your own comfort.

Sit at 3/4 or 1/2 slide, as tall as you can make yourself with your navel drawn into your spine, arms extended with hands and fingers lose and relaxed and your core well connected to the pins through the elbows. When the starting command begins, slightly lean back into the pins. Begin the first stroke by opening your back, then add the legs and arms as you push through the Drive into the pins. Learn the lesson taught by the drill Joy of Backing, that stability comes from working into the blade, not ripping the hands into the bow. Beginning the first stroke as you would a normal stroke with a strong thrust of the legs will absolutely push the boat backwards. Just pry the boat away with your back and then, once inertia has been overcome(that is, once the shell has begun to move forward), you are in familiar territory and you can add legs and arms as you would in a normal stroke. Getting out cleanly is everything.

Unless you are in very rough conditions, be sure not to cut this stroke short at the back end in an effort to get the rating up. That is the purpose of the second stroke.

Second Stroke: this can be very short, 1/2 slide (though 3/4 slide is also effective). Its purpose is to get the rating up. It will feel as though your knees hardly break as you come forward. There is absolutely no need to hurry this. The rating comes up because the stroke is so short. Be patient. Allow the stroke to come to you.

Third Stroke: the purpose of this stroke is to begin to get your length. Now come up to 3/4 slide. Stay relaxed and begin to lengthen out.

Fourth Stroke: continues the purpose of the third, lengthening to 7/8ths of full slide.

Fifth Stroke: by this stroke, you want to be at full slide.

Many scullers follow these five strokes with a series of 10-20 strokes made at a slightly higher rating than the body of your race, and I think this is much more important if you are in a "short" race. If you are racing 1000 meters, you need to get going in a hurry. You do not have a great deal of time to make up distance if you fall a little behind.

If, however, you are racing 2000 meters or more, it is possible to just let your stroke rate 'settle" down to your race cadence naturally within some 6 or 7 strokes. A series of high strokes after the initial five is less important. Settling into your rhythm rather quickly is more important. However, here it comes down to a question of comfort and conditioning.

Starting from a stake boat in a current requires some special considerations. Among other things, starting commands have changed over the years. Make sure you know exactly what the commands will be and how they will be delivered. As of now, they are (with or without a countdown) "Attention (pause of some length, or no pause)...Go". Normally you would have your blades squared before "attention"; however, if you are in a river with a current, you must delay squaring until the "tion" of "attention"; squaring before that will cause your boat to be pulled around, off the stake boat, or into some other disaster.

This brings up another important point about racing...be prepared for all eventualities and expect something to go wrong! You may be late to the starting line, not get your planned warm-up in, clash oars, crab, forget your speed computer, etc.

Suggested Drills:

■ Joy of Backing #5: to learn the absolute importance of always working into the blade so as not to rip the handles into the bow and find yourself suddenly going from lane 3 to lane 5.

Competitive Rowing

Head Racing

Chapter **11**

Conditions. Adjust to the conditions; don't wrestle with them. For example, if you are in a serious head or tail wind with some good chop, don't struggle to hold your rating artificially. Good powerful strokes are more important than rough, high strokes. At the Release, getting out cleanly is even more important in a head or tail wind/chop. Particularly under such conditions, you do not want to be too long at the back end, causing you to get caught at the Release.

The main principle is that, regardless of conditions, you must be RACING. This is both a physical and psychological condition and requires you to be aggressive, thoughtful and, sometimes, patient. For example, let's suppose that the water is quite rough, as it can be in the Charles River Basin in Boston at the start of the Head of The Charles. Sometimes, it is just not possible to get your full length with full power until you have gone under the Boston University Bridge some 45 to 50 seconds into the race. You must shorten up, get out cleanly, push the shell along as best you can and wait until you have passed under the bridge when you can get your full length and power. If this is the case, consciously begin your race here. Be prepared for this tactic from the beginning. In head racing, as in all types of racing, the overriding principle is: expect something to go wrong! Do not stress if and when it does. Plan for it; to race sometimes means being crafty!

The Start. Control your start! Keep as much distance as possible between you and the shell which starts in front of you—no matter how much yelling the Starter does to get you to "bring it up". Stay calm and give yourself more than enough room to be up to full speed before the starting line without putting yourself too close to the shell in front of you. During the paddle toward the line, focus on your breathing pattern. It is a good way to stay calm and helps with your rhythm. Before you have reached the starting line, begin with a full 6 to 7 strokes of a racing start and be certain to be at full racing speed or just a little above before the starting line (assuming, of course, that conditions allow for this). After those 6 or 7 "blast strokes", let the rating settle to your desired rate within the next 6 or 7 strokes.

You can "blast" out of the chute for those 6 or 7 strokes because the metabolic process which supplies the energy here (ATP-CP reaction) is independent of the metabolic process, glycolysis (both anaerobic and aerobic), upon which you will be relying for the remainder of the race. After those initial few strokes, this energy source is used up. Take full advantage of this. A few seconds gained at the start can mean several places at the finish line.

The Body of the Race. Establish your rate and rhythm in a controlled manner. There are two scenarios which must be avoided: "saving yourself" (holding back) and "fly and die". You must have a good knowledge of what rate you can hold for the entire race! Going out too high will cook you before five minutes are up. Even one or two beats above what you are prepared to race could be enough to send you home very disappointed. The important thing is to be racing as hard as you can, not as high as you can.

On the other hand, you need to be on the edge. Just because the race is some three miles long does not mean that it is rowed at anything less than flat out. As long as you are not rowing at a rate too high, you can race at absolutely full pressure. That is the only way to race. Holding back, even a little, will not yield the desired results. The point is, no matter the rating, you must be racing, never holding back, always on the edge. You can do this as long as your rating is not above your desired rate. It is better to be one beat too low than one too high! This is not holding back; it is using your head.

If you have done your preparation, you should be able to race three miles with a rating two to three beats under that which you race for your shorter summer regattas. The best way I know to learn exactly what rating and pace you can hold for a three mile race is to do 7 x 3 min. on with 2 min. off. Begin this workout once or twice a week some two months before your target race. The rating and pace you can hold for those 7 pieces will be what you can do for three miles!

It is useful to know some landmarks on the course, so that you can break it up into smaller bits. Race from one landmark to the next, all the way along the course. Set small goals.

Somewhere around four to five minutes, things get interesting. This is the amount of fatigue and discomfort that you must sustain for the rest of the race. If you are racing, the level of discomfort will not get worse from there until the final moments of the sprint, when it no longer matters. You have to be mentally prepared for this—and determined. That is all there is to it! It really won't get any worse, but you cannot let it to get any easier. (See Chapter13)

Passing. It is very important for you to control your course as much as possible. If you are coming up on someone, you must be confident, positive and forceful. A simple and direct "Coming through" generally works better than a "May I come through?" Any sign of uncertainty or hesitation and the sculler/boat may not give way. Try to learn as much about the people in front of you as possible so you can anticipate what might happen. Whether using a mirror or not, you need to be thinking about 100 yards ahead. Develop the skill of always knowing what is going on ahead of you (as well as behind you). You need to practice this as much as you practice your technique and conditioning. Many races end in disappointment because of ill attention to passing—and steering.

Competitive Rowing

Steering

Chapter 12

Steering is seldom really practiced other than in a functional sort of way; yet it is vital for both safety and preservation of speed. There are two issues to consider: When in the stroke cycle to look around and How to actually negotiate the turning of the boat.

The When. The least desirable, yet most convenient, time to look around is at the Release. This is least desirable because it breaks up the flow of the Follow-Through and the seamless transition from the Drive to the Recovery. This is particularly disruptive in team boats.

The orthodox method is to look around just after the Entry, early in the Drive, when the boat is supposed to be in its most stable condition. However, this not only seems to be the least convenient time, but it requires a good deal of practice before it becomes natural. (See Erging) I find mid-Recovery, after the Follow-Through and the Body Rock, to be the easiest and also the most natural time to look. Simply follow the blades as they travel toward the bow.

When looking, it is not necessary to make a full identification of an object. It is sufficient to simply register "object" in your psyche!

You should look every 5 or 6 strokes, first over one shoulder, then after another 5 or 6 strokes, over the other. A mirror is a great aid, especially in setting a course. However, you absolutely cannot rely upon it to pick up every object that may affect your course; its field of vision is just too small.

The How. I owe much of my advocacy of this technique which I call the Glide Turn to a discussion I had with Cambridge Boat Club sculler, Malcolm Gefter.

While there will be times in a sculling boat when you must call upon the arm on the outside of the turn to reach out a little longer and to draw in a little harder, try as much as possible to keep the pull with each arm equal. Using one over the other is very disruptive and tends to drop the shell down to one side causing the shell to "bank" around the turn, that is, to lean into it. This causes the bow of the boat to plough into the water and the water to "push" back against the hull, dramatically slowing the boat. Your speed just plummets!

Whenever possible, make your turn by using extra force from the leg on the outside of the turn. Any pressure whatsoever from the inside leg will significantly increase the time and distance of the turn. In addition to using only this outside leg, slightly lean into this working leg. This will cause your boat to lean away from the turn and thus to glide around it rather than banking into it and ploughing through it. In this way, the water will actually assist with the turn.

It is interesting to note how little speed you lose in a shell when using only one leg—at least for a short period of time. This is somewhat similar to cycling. Bicycles are, of course, a much more efficient method of transportation. It is therefore fairly easy to sustain your speed on a bicycle when using only one leg, especially on flat ground. Observe how long you can do this while cycling or pedaling on a spinning bike. Now try it on an ergometer.

In a sweep boat, the turns are slightly different. I really prefer to have the side of the boat which is on the inside of the turn to take all the pressure off, rather than have the poor grunts on the outside "pull it around". How disheartening! The only job of those on the outside is to continue doing their splendid rowing. The job of those on the inside, and it is a very important one, is to get their blades in and out exactly with those on the outside. As in your sculling boat, any pressure at all from those on the inside will only increase the time it takes the oarsmen to get around the turn. In addition, having the crew leaning just slightly "away" will produce the desired "glide" effect, rather than the "plough" effect.

Competitive Rowing

Dealing With Intense Mental and Physical Discomfort

Chapter 13

Intense mental and physical discomfort is one of the most defining characteristics of a rowing race and how you deal with it is one of the most significant indicators of the probability of success. It has both physiological and psychological components. There are many very good books that deal with the physiology of training which lead to increased tolerance of pain but are beyond the scope of this book.

However, without a doubt, the biggest psychological asset in helping you deal with this mental and physical distress is simple motivation.

That being said, there are some basic strategies which you can practice which will prepare you to better deal with the stress and strain of rowing. Which you choose is an individual preference. For example, some competitors will focus on the distress; they dive right into it and explore it. Others will focus upon something else; they do not so much ignore the pain as re-direct their attention to something that does not hurt.

A few persons can, in fact, ignore the pain. As Peter O'Toole, speaking as Lawrence of Arabia, said in the movie, "The trick, William Potter, is not minding that it hurts." I have a feeling, however, that this will not work for most of us who, when we try to ignore it, end up just backing off. Those who do not back off, often, are the true champions.

Whatever strategy one chooses, there is one bit of knowledge that I believe will dramatically improve your ability to deal with intense distress. This was taught to me by Jon Kabat-Zinn, Professor of Medicine Emeritus and founding director of the Stress Reduction Clinic and Center for Mindfulness in Medicine, Health Care, and Society at the University of Massachusetts Medical School when he worked with the MIT Heavyweight Crew while I was coaching there. Namely, it is not the distress which is the major problem. Rather, it is the fear that you are not going to be able to continue to tolerate it into the future. This is reminiscent of Franklin Delano Roosevelt's famous statement in his inauguration speech of 1933, "The only thing we have to fear is fear itself". This too echoes the words of the Greek stoic philosopher, Epictetus, who expressed in his Discourses, the wisdom that "it is not pain that is to be dreaded, but the fear of pain".

As Professor Kabat-Zinn wrote to me,"The key principle of dealing mindfully with intense sensation (even labeling it pain is a potential problem) is to embrace it in the present moment, and to recognize that thoughts about future pain (or anything about the future), or how long it is going to last will all cost you energy and are not relevant to the present-moment experience (or winning). They are just thoughts, and when they are seen as such, and not as facts, you automatically, for at least that moment, liberate yourself from their tyrannical, distracting, and therefore disempowering narrative, and the energy drain that ensues. Then we take care of the next moment...and the next...and that moment is always now, always this moment."

The point that you need to recognize is that at any particular time you are, in fact, dealing with the neurological and mental distress, moment to moment. It does not get worse. Deal with this stroke, then the next one...one at a time. Do not look down the road! It is the fear that will cause you to back off, not the discomfort.

Safety

Getting In and Out of Your Shell from a Dock

Chapter **14**

Once the shell is in the water, place your dockside oar into the oarlock with the button pressed against the oarlock and close and fasten the gate. Make sure that the oarlock is facing toward the stern of the boat. The dockside oar goes in first because sometimes you may have to leave your shell briefly for some reason, e.g., to fetch a water bottle, etc. The oar resting upon the dock will help secure the boat while you are gone.

Before placing the other oar into the oarlock, remove your shoes or whatever foot apparel you wore down to the dock. You never want to step into the shell wearing whatever it is that you wore when bringing the boat to the dock. This will bring dirt into the shell.

Now secure the other oar in place and push it out so that the button presses snugly against the oarlock. Next, fasten the gate over the oar. It is easier to fasten this gate if you place one of your knees on the seat deck between the tracks and reach across the boat rather than placing your foot between the tracks. Having your knee on the seat deck drops you down closer to the level of the oarlock, thus shortening the distance you must reach. It also lowers your center of gravity, making the boat more stable.

Standing on the dock with your weight on both feet, bend over and take the oar handles into your hand which is closest to the shell as you face the stern of the shell. With both blades in the feathered position, one floating on the water, the other resting on the dock, butt the face of both

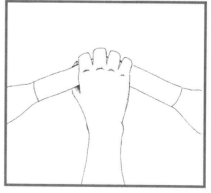

Butt and draw **back**, **not** up or down.

60

handles together, rather than overlap them, and draw them back toward the bow. Butting them together and drawing back secures the buttons against the oarlocks/pins and stabilizes your shell. Overlapping them gives you no such stability.

Your other hand is now free to grab the gunwale, rigger or dock, whichever makes you feel more stable. Keeping your weight on the foot which is furthest dockside from the shell, use your other foot to position the seat toward the bow. Make sure that the shell is sufficiently off the dock that when putting your weight into it, you will not force the hull down onto the edge of the dock. Now, keeping your weight firmly on the supporting leg on the dock, place your free foot into the shell between the tracks. Once in place, shift your weight onto the foot in the boat. Do not find yourself shifting your weight while the free foot in is mid-air. Wait until it is placed in the boat before shifting your weight. While doing this, be sure to continue to draw back the butted oar handles. DO NOT PUSH DOWN ON THE HANDLES. Pushing down on the handles will remove the blades from the water and/or dock and cause the boat to tip to one side or the other. Keep both blades secure and in place. Finally, lower yourself into the boat while using your free hand for support. While lowering yourself, be sure to draw back and not push down!

Getting out of your shell follows the same principles in reverse order. Keep your buttons pressed against the pins by pushing the handles toward your feet, butting the handles together and drawing them back. Use your free, dockside hand for support and with both feet between the tracks draw back on the handles and stand up. A common mistake people often make while standing is pushing down on the handles as though they were going to give you some support. Once again, this will remove the blades from the dock, the water or both and the shell will tip. Once standing with your weight on both feet, place the dockside foot onto the dock and then shift all your weight onto the dock. Now you can bring the other foot and waterside oar across the boat and onto the dock.

The same method is used for getting in and out even if you do not have a dock and must use either the shore or bottom of river or lake. Keep your handles butted and draw back while you step in or out.

Safety

Getting Back Into (or Onto) Your Shell from the Water

Chapter 15

There are two methods for doing this. One is rather difficult for many people and requires both good upper body strength and practice—I call this the Hoist-over-the Gunwale Method. In addition, some shells are much easier to get into than others. The other is much more reliable under any and all conditions and is considerably easier—**I call this the Harbor Seal on the Deck Method.** (See Cold Water Rowing)

The most difficult and, curiously, in the United States most taught method, is the Hoist-Over-the-Gunwale Method. To begin, position yourself on the side of the boat which will allow you to use your dominant arm to push yourself up into the boat. This would be the starboard side if you are right-handed, port if left-handed. Push the oar handles into the stern so that they can be butted together and hold them with your less dominant hand and pull them back

toward the bow, forcing the buttons against the pins. Pull the handles down into the bottom of the boat and tip the shell down onto the side nearest you such that the oar away from you is up in the air. Make sure that the oar which is now on the water is feathered and on the surface of the water.

Melanie Rovens

Harbor Seal on the Deck

Get **as much** of **yourself** as possible **out of the water.**

Now, place your dominant hand on the seat deck behind the seat and with one good scissors kick and a strong push from your arm, hoist yourself up and spin your body to face the stern. With luck, you will land on the seat while your legs are still in the water on the side of the shell. As you do this, lift the handles so that the shell levels itself and both blades rest upon the water and you have some stability. Lastly, swing your feet into the shell—and presto!

Clearly, this is a difficult maneuver and many people simply cannot do it. Furthermore, what is doable in warm water in July may not be doable in November and attempting to do so (in the belief that you can) could cost you your life.

This is why I prefer the Harbor Seal on the Deck Method.

If your intent is to get back in right there and row away, you must first gather the oar handles together and bring them into the bow. Then get yourself to the bow and pull yourself up onto it and make your way towards the cockpit. When close enough to grab the oars do so with one hand and then pull yourself up with your legs along each side until you are sitting up. Now get yourself up and over the wash box and into the boat, keeping the blades flat on the water.

Before choosing which method by which you can re-mount your boat while you are still out in the middle of the river/lake, you must decide exactly what your goals are. If you are not too far from the shore and the shore has an accessible landing spot, you may simply maneuver yourself to either the bow or stern of your boat and pull yourself up onto the deck. You can then "paddle" yourself to shore as if on a surfboard.   Similarly, if you are in an older shell and have concerns for the durability of the gunwales or wash box, you also might consider this method of simply lying on the deck and paddling with your arms to shore.

Safety

Cold Water Rowing

Chapter 16

Education and common sense are the two most important factors in dealing with cold water situations. Being immersed in cold water is frightening. Body heat is lost at an alarming rate. The body cools off some 25 times faster in water than in air. This is especially dangerous for athletes who have little body fat. Survival time varies according to age, gender, body size, weight and general health. These factors should be taken into consideration before one decides to go for a row in cold water situations.

When you are immersed in cold water, nerve activity and muscle movement ability diminish very quickly. Your external body temperature ("shell temperature") drops much faster than your internal, core temperature. Therefore, your brain may be fine initially, but your ability to hold onto something will not be. This is one of the biggest dangers: a rower believes he/she can do things such as hold on to a boat or swim distances that in normal conditions would seem easy, but, under these conditions, are not.

People rarely die of hypothermia—they drown! The main reason for this is that they cannot hold onto whatever flotation they have. In 40 degree water, grip strength dissipates in 15 minutes or less.

Another reason people drown is Sudden Disappearance Syndrome. Someone falls in and just sinks. The cold water causes an involuntary contraction of the diaphragm causing the subject to exhale forcefully. The natural response to this is to inhale immediately after the forced exhale and thereby to take in water. This same syndrome will also make it difficult for you to hold your breath; so don't try to swim under the boat. The danger of this syndrome can last from three to five minutes. In addition, your rate of breathing will be more rapid and shallow. You should anticipate these problems and stay calm.

When confronted with sudden immersion in cold water, first, get your head above water! Second, get ahold of your boat and begin to get as much of your body out of the water as possible. It is probably better to use the Harbor Seal on the Deck Method rather than the Hoist over the Gunwale Method under these circumstances. The hoist method could well exhaust you and leave you incapable of pursuing any other options. Whatever you decide to do, figure that you have only one chance. Do not hold anything back. Once on top of your boat, collect your thoughts. Try to conserve energy.

How far you are from shore should determine whether you try to maneuver your boat by either kicking (if unable to get on top of the boat) or rowing; or leaving your boat and swimming. It has been a common practice and often taught as dogma to never leave your boat. However, this will do you no good if you cannot hold on to your boat. Remember, in 40 degree water you have no more than 15 minutes to hold onto anything.

Use Common Sense! If you do opt to swim for it, never try to swim to shore without flotation! If you do not have a personal flotation device (pfd) either on you or in the boat, place one oar under each arm for support. In case you didn't know it, your oars will float!

Take cold weather/water very seriously! Here is a check list:

■ Find and wear a personal flotation device (pfd) which will allow you to row comfortably. There are any number of these available.

■ Bring your cell phone enclosed in a waterproof bag. And add some flotation to the bag. The phone won't do you any good if it is at the bottom of the river/lake.

■ Have an extra set of warm clothes, which you can change into back at the boat house.

■ Arrive at the boathouse prepared to handle the possibility that you may get wet.

■ Row with others if possible.

Training

Erging

Chapter **17**

When it comes to the ergometer, technique often goes out the window as soon as butt meets seat. Some people take more strokes on an ergometer than they do on the water. Therefore, while erging, it is important that you try to reinforce proper technique as much as you can in a two dimensional world without a pin.

On the other hand, if you are in an erg race or a situation which requires you to attain a particular score, hold your nose and, as they say, "Just Do It". Erg score is all about Force x Distance. Therefore, pulling the handles up to your eyes, huge layback, no "Release", rushing up the slide all may well help your score. On the water, of course, these techniques will kill your speed.

Just because there is no pin and you cannot, therefore, apply pressure through your elbows into it, does not mean that there are not numerous technical aspects of the stroke that you can work on.

The Release and Recovery. Focus on your posture, your Follow-Through and the path of your handle. With your trunk firm and still, hinge the "Release" from the elbows (Mantle). On the Follow-Through, keep your elbows out and on the same horizontal plane. Your hands come away first parallel to your belly and then parallel to your thighs until past your knees and then continue parallel to the floor. From there until the "Entry", the hands should remain at the same height. As in rowing on the water, your body angle should be completed with your arms fully extended before the knees come up and the seat moves. During the second half of the Recovery, your hands and seat should be traveling at the same speed.

The Drive. Here the chain must travel in a slight arching path from leaving the sprocket until the finish of the Drive, following your center of gravity. This is easy to observe.

Do not let your elbows drop. Keep then pointing outward with your shoulders rolled forward.

Do not bring the handle way up your chest or get exaggerated layback even though this will give you a better score. These are habits you will carry out onto the water. If you need a particular score to make a seat in a boat or for some other reason, do what you need to do, but do not train in this manner.

Other Technical Aspects. Erging does offer a good opportunity to work on Breathing, looking around as if Steering, and the Glide Turn. Practice taking some strokes with only one leg and try to maintain speed while you lean slightly into the working leg. **Give it a try!**

One last word on erging. I cannot recommend enough getting a "Shox-Box". See **www.shoxbox.biz**. This is a suspension box which is placed under the rear legs of the erg. It serves to absorb the impact of your weight coming down onto your lower back at the end of a stroke. When rowing, the water absorbs and cushions this impact. A floor does not. This device will really help preserve your back from all that stress.

Training

Some Drills for Maximizing the Ease of Sculling (and Sweep Rowing) in a Nutshell

Chapter 18

The best way to improve your rowing, to make these movements habits, is to do Drills. Generally, do a drill for a certain period of time and then follow this by rowing easily trying to implement the lesson of the drill before moving on to another drill. Try something like 5 strokes of the drill followed by 5 strokes imagining that you are doing the drill and then do 5 strokes of easy rowing. Repeat until satisfied with the execution. Keep the number of drills you will work on each day to a minimum. Either doing too many strokes of a drill or too many drills makes it very difficult to keep your mind focused.

"King of the Mountain" #1 (a progression drill)

■ Square Release:

Sitting at the back end of the Drive, legs flat, hands at center of gravity near your body where you make the Release and wrists flat. The elbows are out and in front of your body and level with the hands. Your shoulders are down and rolled forward; your core is stable; and your navel is drawn into your spine. You are A Fortress of Stability. Apply an exaggerated force against the pin toward the blade with your triceps, pectoral muscles, and especially your elbows in an almost isometric exercise pushing toward the pins/blades.

Keep a vertical orientation, i.e., your weight should be above the handles and the major muscles of your back should be drawn down onto the riggers. Begin tapping the blades half way out of the water using your entire forearms hinged at the elbows (your entire core). Hold your elbows steady with a stable shoulder girdle. Make sure your shoulders are rolled forward (stabilizing your shoulder girdle). You should feel as though you were beginning to lift yourself out of a pool by pressing down on the pool deck (Mantling). Once you have established stability and some rhythm, bring the blades all the way out, still fully squared. Do not use your wrists to extract the blades from the water. Then, after you re-establish your stability and rhythm, make three more releases and, on the last one, release and feather, again being sure to come out of the water with blades squared. Keep your wrists flat and keep the extraction and the feathering as separate events. Do this until stable and then proceed to...

■ Release, Feather, Hands Away:

While still maintaining your core stability and feeling as though you were lifting yourself out of the pool (Mantling), hinge the release from stationary elbows using your forearms, etc. Feather and begin to swing your hands away keeping them on as close to the same plane as possible.

Follow this symmetrical pattern: down parallel to your belly and then down towards your knees parallel to your thighs with the space between your second and third knuckles of your trailing hand (See Release) brushing the base of the thumb of the leading hand. Once the arms are straight, PAUSE. Do not move your body; remain stable in your layback position. Repeat the drill until satisfied and stable. Your goal should be to be able to pause with the hands away with both blades off the water and your boat stable. This does not require that you be one of the rowing gods. It only requires that you practice, over and over. Once you can pause with your arms away and the blades off the water and feathered, you can progress into doing a Newton, Drill #7. The stroke and your stability begin at the Release. It must be perfect.

(One of the most important purposes of this drill is developing the ability to swing the arms away without losing the pressure against the pin. Guard against letting the shell drop to one side or the other. This is caused by losing the pin as the elbows come closer together on the Follow-Through. There should be very little change in the horizontal plane of the elbows throughout this entire drill. The forearms hinge down, but the elbows remain on the same plane as they lead the hands away. "Release the Frisbee".)

Pause Drills #2

These drills are extremely versatile. You can use them to isolate many parts of the Recovery or the Drive.

■ Arms Away:

After executing the correct Release of the blade from the water, brace the trunk and legs and "release the frisbee". Then pause with the trunk still and the hands away and the legs flat. Be absolutely certain not to lose the connection to the pins as the arms swing away. The arms should be extended, but not rigid, and the shoulders should be rolled forward and the elbows slightly rolled upward. The trunk is still "in the bow" and the elbows are firmly working into the pins. This should be done without any movement whatsoever of the back. When sculling, check that the hands are as close to the same plane as possible with the left or starboard ever so slightly above and ahead of the right. Make sure you have maintained firm contact with the pins through the elbows (See King of the Mountain). Check the pattern and be sure that the space between the second and third knuckles of the following hand has brushed the base of the thumb of the leading hand.

After a momentary pause, rotate the pelvis, relax the belly and continue the Recovery and stroke until the next Release. The path of the hands is parallel to the body (on the Release), then parallel to the thighs (on the Follow -Through), and finally, once the hands have passed over the knees, parallel to the water as you spread out to make the Entry. Be absolutely assiduous as to not letting the pressure come off the pins or the elbows drop during the Follow-Through. (See King of the Mountain)

■ Arms Away and Body Over:

After the Follow-Through make sure that you have released your knees and that they are no longer "locked". Keep your spine straight yet flexible, like a stalk of bamboo, your chest up and your latissimus dorsi (lats) muscles drawn down onto the riggers. Now, rotate your pelvis and pause. (See "Swans", drill, #6) Then continue up the slide through your normal stroke. Feel the acceleration of the shell caused by the "rock" (rotation) of the hips. (See Rock & Row)

■ Half-Slide Pause:

Having executed the initial part of the Recovery and established your body angle with your weight riding the riggers and the pins, pause your slide movement at half-slide. (We can consider having the angle between the back of your thighs and your calf muscles at 45 degrees as constituting the half-slide position.) Observe how it is that you came to a pause. You pause by ceasing to separate your handles, not by pushing on the foot plate. Check hand/handle position and be sure to maintain your pressure on the pin. Keeping a "long neck" and chest up and navel drawn into your spine, after a momentary pause, continue on to the Entry and the rest of the stroke until the next pause at half-slide. Your upper body preparation and arm extension

(Reach) should be accomplished before the seat begins to move. If your seat begins to move before your arms are straight or your proper body angle has been attained, the only way you will be able to move the seat is with your legs drawing you forward. (See Skimming, drill #4)

If sculling, your full length is accomplished in the time after the pause by continuing to separate the distance between the handles right up to and through the Entry. If sweeping, the full length comes during the second half of the Recovery by continuing to swivel the oar around the pin. Make a distinction between the first half of the Recovery, when you are establishing your reach, and the second half, when you are moving yourself into the stern by applying pressure against the pin toward the blades (establishing your Length). Feel as though you are in a state of neutrality relative to the movement of the boat.

When doing this drill, there are a number of things you can focus on beyond basic body preparation. One particularly important aspect is to pay attention to what is happening as you come into and out of the pause. Make certain that you do not stop yourself (pause) by placing your weight against the foot stretcher. In other words do not use your legs to stop your movement into the stern. Your movement into the stern during the Recovery is controlled by your ARMS, not your Legs. The Recovery is 100% upper body. Pause by stopping the separation of your handles. Then check your connection to the pins. Are you supported by the riggers with your chest up, lats drawing your weight up off your feet and off your seat? Is your weight distributed onto the riggers and therefore throughout the entire shell? Check these points! Then continue your movement into the stern/Entry by a resumption of the separation of the handles, again, not by pulling yourself up the slide with your legs.

"Rock and Row" #3

Pause with hands away. Then "rock" by rotating your hips and establish your body angle. After a momentary pause, on the command "row", proceed up the slide into the Entry and onto the Drive. This is a great drill for establishing rhythm in a team boat, and for feeling the acceleration of the shell as you rock out of bow. (See velocity curve)

"Skimming" #4

This drill is designed to help you learn the method of propelling yourself into the stern and making the Entry without using your legs or feet to draw yourself forward. It teaches you how to stay off your feet during the Recovery. It is one of the most important, yet one of the easiest drills. Because using your legs to draw yourself into the stern is so ingrained, so much a part of what you think the Recovery entails, you should practice this a couple times a day. A good time is whenever you turn around. Do it once or twice an outing. That is all you need.

■ From the Body Over:

Begin at the back end of the Follow-Through with your arms straight and body rocked over. With your oars lying flat on the surface of the water, release your knees and begin to draw yourself up the slide as though you were sitting on a skate board in a doorway (sliding pocket doors) and you could pull yourself through it by using only your arms as you apply pressure against the door frame/pins in the direction that the imaginary blades are moving. During this exercise, focus on your connection to the pins through your elbows, weight off the feet and distributed throughout the boat on the riggers. You can go through the same checklist as during the Half-Slide Pause Drill. (# 2). Remember, the recovery is 100% upper body!

■ From 3/4 Slide:

Sit at 3/4 slide with your body angle and arm extension complete and ready for the last 1/4 of the slide into the Entry with your blades feathered and resting on the surface of the water. From this point, by separating the handles (or swiveling the handle around the pin for sweep rowing), propel yourself forward by drawing the seat and your still, stable body toward the stern. Stay off your feet! Avoid pulling yourself up by your feet, rather, use the pressure on the pin as the handle swivels outward to propel yourself. Keep your sternum up! (In a sweep boat, it is the inside arm which propels you into the stern as you swivel around the pin. The outside arm takes care of the blade placement.)

■ Combined with the Half-Slide Pause Drill:

A very instructive variation of this skimming drill is to pause at half-slide. This, better than any drill I know, makes you aware of when your weight is on your feet and therefore on the foot stretcher. Observe how it is that you came to this Pause at 1/2 slide. It should have been by ceasing to separate your arms, not by pushing against the foot stretcher. After the pause, continue up to what would be the Entry. Return and repeat.

By doing this drill you will come to realize how prevalent it is that you stop your forward movement by pressing against the foot stretcher, thereby checking the run of the boat.

"Joy of Backing" #5

One of the most important lessons of this drill is that it is the pressure into the pin in the direction the blade is moving that gives you stability.

■ The Basic Drill:

Sit at the back end of the Drive/the Release with your legs flat and blades squared in the water. Back by pushing your handles away and let them lead you up the slide with relaxed legs and soft hands. As you approach the stern (where you would be making the Entry), feel the water begin to pull the blades toward the bow, the handles into your finger tips and you into the stern.

When you have been pulled to where you would be making the Entry, pause a moment, turn the upper tips of your blades toward your feet (reverse feather) and, letting the blades skim along the surface, return to your starting position at the back end of the Drive. Repeat this backing exercise until you are quite comfortable with the feeling of being pulled into the stern.

At first, this being pulled forward is rather unsettling. Once comfortable with this feeling of being pulled, you will discover that it is the technique of always pushing into the blade, working with the blades, not resisting them that gives you stability. Always work your pressure into the blades.

■ Adding the Drive:

Once you are comfortable with this feeling, pause briefly at what would be the "Entry" and then complete the stroke by executing a Drive. It is absolutely vital that you do not rip the handles into the bow as though you were on an ergometer. If you are to avoid the possibility of being flipped into the water, you must drive into the pins! We are after the feeling of the water accepting your blades and the stable, secure feel of the blades being locked onto the water. This gives you the idea of how the Drive develops without ripping the handles toward you by working with the water with soft hands. Tension in the hands and pulling the handles towards yourself will give you a very unstable feeling. The key is to apply pressure against the pins toward the blades while you are being drawn forward during the backing and while you are on the Drive.

After you can comfortably do one good backing stroke followed by a Drive, then proceed to doing three consecutive strokes after the backing stroke. Remember, always work into the blades. You are now rowing (in a nutshell).

This is a great drill to practice your Starts. Learn the lessons of this drill and you will avoid starting in lane three and ending up in lane two or four after the first stroke of a racing start. The key is working into the blades, not pulling on the handles.

"Swans" #6

This drill should probably be done outside the shell. Its purpose is to teach the correct method of rotating your pelvis when setting your body angle after the Follow-Through.

It can be done either standing or while seated. If standing, relax your knees. Your hips do not rotate freely if your knees are locked. Hold your arms straight out from your sides with your palms facing toward the front. Holding your head up with a nice long neck and your spine straight, bend forward from your waist. Holding your arms out helps to keep your chest up and your spine straight, putting the emphasis on the rotation of the pelvis. If seated, release your knees and with your arms out and palms forward, rotate your pelvis.

"Newtons" #7

This drill is so named for Isaac Newton's Third Law of Motion. The purpose of this drill is to increase your awareness of the movement of the shell and your effect upon this movement during the Recovery and Entry.

Begin at the Release position with your blades square and covered in the water. Mantle the blades out. Then follow through and swing the body forward, continuing the Recovery into the stern. Feel the effect of your body mass moving toward the stern setting the shell in motion in the opposite direction. Be sure that it is the pressure against the pin(s) out and back which is moving you into the stern, not your legs drawing the boat under you. Your legs should remain completely relaxed! (See Recovery) The Entry should be executed without interrupting this movement, without any pressure upon the foot stretcher or force upon the blade as it enters the water. Make the Entry by continuing to have the handles swivel around the pin and pushing the blade down. Allow the water to stop the blade.

Every effort should be made to keep the shell and your body stable by maintaining constant and equal pressure on the oarlock and keeping your hands in the same relative position. Always be drawing your major back muscles down onto the riggers. Stabilize! Do not try to balance the boat. Once the water has taken the blades, relax, reverse feather the blades out of the water and return to the Release position by skimming the oars on the surface of the water. And repeat the drill.

"Front End" #8

The purpose of this drill is to teach you to feel the effect of the water on the loaded and anchored blade, so that you will know how to move the boat—immediately. It is not about bringing the handles anywhere. The boat should feel heavy and MOVE!

Begin at 3/4 slide. Use the pressure against the pins toward the blade and the separation of your handles to propel yourself into the stern. Ride the riggers. Stay off your feet. Bury the blade while still separating the hands (or, for sweep rowing, while still swiveling) and drive the first 1/4th of the Drive. Then release the water and pause. There are a number of points to keep in mind here: (1) keep the horizon flat as you bury the blade and begin the Drive; (2) don't let your head or chest drop,; (3) keep your legs relaxed during the Recovery through the Entry; and, of course, (4) stay off your feet!

You will want to expand your chest (inhale) as you make the Entry. The distance between your hands and your body, on the one hand, and your hands and the seat, on the other hand, should not change through the entire movement, all the way from the last 1/4th of the Recovery, through Entry and into the first 1/4th of the Drive! Every effort should be made to maintain this distance between the seat/body and the handle. The movement into the stern should be accomplished by using the pressure against the pin to propel you forward through the Entry. Do not use your feet to draw yourself forward or to place the blade into the water. (See Half Slide Pause drill, #2C and Skimming, #3) Once the blade is in the water, think of moving the boat, not the blade. Drive into the blade.

After a few strokes, continue without a pause for a number of strokes and finally, row the stroke out with full length drives. These final strokes should be close to perfect. If you are in a team boat, this can be done as a progression drill, going from one or two rowers taking a number of strokes with a pause at hands—away at Release and then adding another one or two more rowers, pausing again after the initial 1/4th of the Drive. This can be continued until the entire boat is doing the drill. The more rowers doing the drill, the more difficult it becomes.

"Blending The Drive" #9

The purpose of this drill is to improve the efficiency of the Drive and avoid wasting energy trying to suddenly accelerate the boat as the arms join the legs and back.

Begin by rowing a number of strokes using just the legs without either the back or the arms joining in. Push off the ball joint of your big toe. Pause at the Release. Next row a number of strokes adding the back right after the hips have engaged (when the heels have snapped down and you have a stable platform). This time, pause after the Release with the arms away. Finally, add the arm draw somewhere in the final third of the Drive, just as you feel your weight start to settle on the seat. Pause after the Follow-Through/Body Preparation and let the boat decelerate. The focus of this drill is on the point of unification of the arms with the legs and back. This should be accomplished without jerking the arms. It should be smooth and fluid with every effort made to keep constant pressure on the pin and foot stretcher during the Drive and therefore on the blade.

The next phase of the drill is to execute this motion without the pause. The shell will now be traveling much faster and the unification will be more difficult to accomplish smoothly. Work for this seamless blending and a feeling during the Drive of constant pressure on the foot stretcher, pin and blade while holding your suspension right through until the Release.

Points to emphasize while doing this drill:

■ The back should begin to open as soon as the heels have pushed down onto the foot stretcher.

■ The arms should begin the draw the instant that you feel your body weight begin to settle onto the seat. At this point of the Drive, biomechanically, your arms and upper body are a match for your legs in strength and can continue your "unweighted suspension" through to the Release.

(An interesting variant of this drill is to do it on an ergometer. Just work on the smooth blend of the unification motion. Keep your eyes on the chain as it comes off the sprocket and, keeping it in the upper third of the window, make sure that it travels in a path following your center of gravity to the point just below your sternum at your center of gravity. Notice that this should transcribe a gentle arc, as your center of gravity changes relative to the floor.)

"Feet Out" #10

The purpose of this drill is to increase your ability to keep constant pressure on your foot stretcher, pin and blade during the Drive and to learn where the proper release point of the Drive is.

Remove your feet from the shoes or clogs and row. This drill gives you immediate feedback on how well you are blending the legs, back and arms and continuing a smooth acceleration. You should strive to have your legs, back and arm draw finish at the same time. Any continuation of the stroke, either by back-swing or arm-draw after the legs are done will result in your body falling into the bow of the boat and your feet coming well off the foot stretcher.

Because of your momentum toward the bow caused by the Drive, your feet will naturally come slightly off the stretcher at the Release. Every effort should be made to minimize this by releasing just as the legs and back finish.

One's stability at the Release can be aided by exhaling and using the breath to lift your rib cage as it passes through your body. (See Breathing) Some people have difficulty doing this drill because it hurts their backs. Increasing your stability through proper breathing, especially the exhale at the Release, can help with this. In addition, be sure that your navel is "drawn" into your spine at all times.

When first beginning this drill, make the Release when the hands are clearly further from your body than usual and the blade clearly "loaded" with the vortex solidly behind the blade so that you have a definite reference point for what stability means with your feet remaining on the foot stretcher. Then, over a few strokes, increase your length through the arm-draw at the end of the Drive to the point of "tumbling into the bow". This is when you will know you that either your arm-draw or your body-swing (or both) has gone too far after the completion of the leg drive. Work toward unifying the back end of the Drive so that all of its components—leg-drive, body-swing and arm-draw—conclude at as close to the same time as possible.

Having your feet come off the foot stretcher about 1/2 inch is acceptable; beyond that is not. Keeping your elbows in front of your body and feeling as though they were "changing direction" as they work into the blade will help you get the blades out at the correct time.

"Truncating" #11

This is another progression drill similar to the Blending drill. It is designed to teach the proper feeling of the blade coming out of the water at the correct time and the feeling of releasing from the pressure of a "loaded blade". As with the Blending drill, it progresses from pauses to continuous strokes, thereby increasing both the speed of the boat and the difficulty of proper execution of the drill. It is excellent as a "team boat" drill.

Begin by taking single strokes and pausing with the hands away. The Release should be made just before the legs have finished and before your weight has settled upon the seat. Your legs will not yet be quite straight. (See Radical Finishectomy drill, #17)

It is important to understand that THIS IS NOT A NO-ARMS DRILL! Therefore, although the handles will not be at their normal Release position, the arm-draw should most definitely have begun. In other words, the Drive is "truncated," shortened.

You should be releasing the blade when you are clearly still "suspended" with your hands, perhaps, some 6-8 inches from your body and while you are clearly still using your mass to move the boat. Release the blade from the water just before your weight has settled on the seat, which is before the backs of your knees have hit the seat deck. Releasing at this point (with your hands some 6-8 inches from your body) will cause your blades to absolutely leap out of the water.

After 5-10 of these strokes, each with a pause, bring the arm-draw to full completion of the Drive, releasing just as the leg-drive is completed. Strive for the same feeling of the oars "leaping out". Then do 5-10 strokes without the pause and work for the smooth blending of the draw and releasing at the proper point and search for that feel of the oars coming out effortlessly.

If this is being done in a team boat, have another rower (or group of rowers, if sweeping) join in the drill, picking it up at the completion of the truncated Drive with a pause. The added rowers will be joining the original rowers in repeating the first segment with the truncated Drive. Continue the progression until you have half the boat rowing full strokes with a pause.

Then have the other members of the boat—who have just been sitting there—join in. At this point, the entire boat will be working at a full Drive with a pause. Continue the progression until all are rowing without a pause.

For example, if you are working with an eight, the stern four should do five strokes truncated with a pause, then #3 & 4 join in for five strokes truncated with a pause. Then the bow pair should join in for five strokes truncated with a pause. Next, all eight do five full strokes with a pause. The end of the progression of this drill should have the entire boat rowing full strokes without a pause—and the boat should be flying! Finally, repeat the drill beginning from the bow four.

"Sub-10 Strokes per Minute" #12

The purpose of this drill is to increase your sensitivity to all aspects of the stroke cycle. The low rating makes it necessary to make every movement efficiently and precisely. There should be no pauses or jerks. The drill consists of rowing for a period of time at a sub-10 rating per minute. Everything should flow: Release to Recovery, to Entry, to Drive. And back to Release. Your focus should be on Stability, not Balance.

"Square Blades" #13

The purpose of this drill, which is just rowing without feathering, is to emphasize the extraction of the blade without using your wrist to get the blade out of the water. The extraction should be made by Mantling, using your whole forearm hinged at the elbow while keeping the wrist flat (See Release). As this can be rather frustrating when you are first learning this skill, I suggest alternating 5 strokes square with 5 strokes feathered. Be attentive to releasing with squared blades when you alternate to feathering. That is the point of the drill! It amazes me how often I see someone doing square blade rowing and, when he/she stops the drill, going right back to feathering the blade out of the water.

"Running Down Hill" #14

The purpose of this drill is to develop your skill of rowing at higher rates and to become aware of at what rate your stroke falls apart and what to do when this happens. It is excellent for teaching the importance of never "losing" the pins. When this happens, you have the feeling of being disconnected from the boat and "chasing after it". Your speed drops.

It should also impress upon you that rating should always be directly related to boat speed.

Begin by rowing at full pressure at, perhaps, 3–4 beats under your standard race pace. Then begin to increase your rating every stroke, at first going up by one beat per stroke and then when you can no longer go up by 1 beat go up for 1/2 beat per stroke. Using your speed computer, continue to raise the rating until your speed no longer increases with the increase in rate, or your rate no longer increases. Give yourself 3 strokes during which either the speed does not increase or the rating does not go up. Then paddle, collect yourself, rest and begin again.

There are two main reasons why either the rating or the speed, or both, stop increasing. Either you have begun to put pressure on the foot stretcher before the blade is "loaded", therefore checking (slowing) the boat, or you have lost the pins and therefore lost your frame connection to the riggers during the Follow-Through. This causes you to have the feeling of "chasing" after the boat. When you maintain your frame connection to the riggers, you have all the time you need to do whatever needs to be done!

"Ultra-Wide Grip" #15

This is a drill for sweep rowing only. The purpose of this drill is to encourage you to establish your length by continuing to rotate your trunk and swivel the handle around the pin through the Entry and to give you the feeling of the division of labor between the inside and outside arms during the Recovery, through the Entry and into the Drive.

It also shows you how to make the Recovery without using your legs to pull yourself up the slide. (See Skimming Drill #4)

Move your inside hand well down the loom (shaft) and row long strokes. Use your inside arm through the elbow to push into the blade as you swivel around the pin. This pressure into the blade will propel you up the slide without the using your feet.

As you continue to swivel around the pin with the inside arm propelling you forward, "push" the blade into the water with the outside arm/hand.

The Drive begins with the bulk of the load being carried by the outside arm and gradually evens out as you approach the back end when the inside elbow is pushing forcefully into the blade. (See Appendix: Sweep Rowing compared with Sculling)

This is also an excellent drill for increasing your length at the Entry. Observe where your handle is at the Entry after you have completed the rotation around the pin.

When you return to your regular hand positions, there is no good reason why you should not be able to replicate this length. The thing which will prevent you from attaining the same length is having a rigid inside arm. This prevents you from swiveling as far as you can. It is necessary to keep a slight bend in your inside arm so you can get your full angular rotation, i.e., length.

"Paddle light" #16

"

That means to row each stroke absolutely true but with as little work as possible. This is the hardest exercise to do correctly, and the most beneficial. Each rower should try to come forward with perfect ease at absolute rest. Also he should try to hold the oar balanced evenly on the rowlock and held on the feather till right forward...Let him feel that he springs off the stretcher very lightly but with a true spring with the whole weight; and let him feel that he is drawing with elastic arms at the oar, so as to draw the oar gently but continuously against the rowing pin, and to draw the blade similarly through the water, right to the finish; and then, with a slightly harder pull at the finish, let him whip the oar round the turn. It should all be done with the utmost care. The oarsman should come forward at rest and rock himself on to the stretcher as if he was rocking a baby to sleep, and all through the stroke he should move as if he was nursing a baby to sleep. Thus he will improve his touch rapidly, and that is everything. Perfect the 'Paddle Light' and you perfect your rowing, but it will take a lot of hard trying. **"**

—The Complete Steve Fairbairn on Rowing, Pg. 427

I include this quote from Fairbairn because it is lovely and gives one the sense of how delicate one's movements should be, even though he is placing a different emphasis on some aspects of the stroke and uses terms and methods which are contrary to the ideas of this book. It is an excellent drill and I believe he is correct when he states, "This is the hardest exercise to do correctly, and the most beneficial...Perfect the 'Paddle Light' and you perfect your rowing, but it will take a lot of hard trying."

"Half-Buried Blades" #17

Attempting to row with your blades half-buried has a couple very important effects. First, I have observed that most people go too deep with their blades during the Entry. Watch your blades from the Entry through to the Release and try to keep them only half- buried. (Note, however, that your blades will naturally go a little deeper during the Drive when you open your back. This will properly happen if your handles continue to follow your center of gravity.)

Once you have learned the proper blade depth at the Entry (only the blade should be in the water with almost no shaft or loom), you can begin to try to actually bury the blade only half- way. This exercise will help you develop the skill of working with the water. This requires developing a feel for the speed of the boat and working with it. If you are too impatient, you will tear the blade through the water.

Few can do this at first. You will eventually discover that when you think that your blade is in at half-depth, your blade is, at best, at its proper depth. And, by the way, observe how little effort you have to put into lifting your hands (open the angle of your armpits) to make the Entry.

"Radical Finishectomy" #18

Ah, yes, in case you forgot, **there is no Finish!** However, as this is the conclusion of the Nutshell, I must tell you that I decided long ago that the only way to give lip service to the conventional wisdom about the "finish" would be to re-define what it is all about. So, this drill is similar to our Truncating drill (#11). Make the Release before the backs of the knees have hit the seat deck. Then execute the Follow-Through and pause. Do not worry where your hands are relative to your body when you make the Release. However, as in the truncating drill, this is not a no-arms drill. Make sure that you have begun the final arm-draw and simply make the Release before the legs have hit the deck, i.e. while your legs are still clearly pushing. Observe how the Release feels. This is how it should feel all the time. You will see that you are probably making the Release very close to where it actually should be made. There is no finish!

Happy Sculling! And remember —

The proof is in the puddle!

Appendix

The Principles
of the Nutshell
Applied to Sweep Rowing
Compared to Sculling

Sweep rowing and sculling have basically the same technique.
There are, however, some critical differences which are mostly caused by the fact that sweep rowing, where each person has only one oar, is asymmetrical. Instead of both hands behaving in the same manner, the inside hands and outside hands have different functions and, therefore, different movements. This is especially evident at the Entry and during the Release/Follow-Through and to a lesser degree during the Recovery and Drive.

At the back end of the Drive, the outside hand in a sweep boat rotates outward. The rower's main contact with the oar handle is accomplished with the index and middle fingers. This keeps a straight line between the hand, wrist and elbow. The outside elbow is extended out from the body. As in sculling, the outside elbow is in front of the body and the shoulders (both outside and inside) are "rolled" slightly forward and down, and the wrist is flat. The weight stays above the oar handle.

Except for the fact that the rower uses only the outside arm, the Release is executed with the same motion as in sculling; it is executed by hinging the forearm at the elbow. Once the extraction of the blade is accomplished, the inside hand feathers the blade by lowering the third and raising the second knuckles, without dropping the wrist.

The outside hand/wrist remains flat and the handle simply rotates within the curled hand. Then, in a seamless transition from the Drive to Release/Follow-Through, the outside hand leads the handle away in the same pattern as sculling. As in sculling, it is important to learn to do this with as little movement of the wrists as possible.

The Follow-Through is one of the components of sweeping that is much easier than sculling. This is because the elbows do not come in towards each other while the arms are swinging away, and, thus, there should be no problem with losing the pin.

The sequence of the Recovery is exactly the same as for sculling. The arms swing away with a still, braced, stable trunk (our Fortress of Stability). The pattern of the motion is the same: parallel to the belly at the extraction, parallel to the thighs on the Follow-Through and parallel to the water once the seat has begun to move toward the stern. The body swings forward by the same rotation of the pelvis and the knees come up only after the Reach and Body Preparation are complete.

As in sculling, the rower does not use his/her legs or feet to draw into the stern. You use the same method of applying pressure against the pin in the direction the blade is moving to propel yourself forward into the stern. However, as you swivel around the pin, the pressure is applied to the pin with only the inside arm. Again, the Recovery is 100% upper body and requires you to keep the major muscles of your back drawn onto the rigger. Your weight is above the handle, light on the seat and off the feet.

Your upper body follows the arc of the oar and your trunk rotates to keep the chest more or less parallel to the oar. As with sculling, you are applying pressure against the pin with your entire core, in the direction the blade is moving. Your hands are loose and soft. There is no lean out of the boat. Every effort should be made to keep firm pressure of the button against the oarlock during the entire Recovery, through the Entry of the blade into the water and during the entire Drive.

As your arms straighten and you begin to swivel around the pin, it is necessary to keep a slight bend in the elbow of the inside arm. This will allow you to get significantly more angular rotation and therefore length.

You need to follow the same principle of stabilizing the boat rather than trying to "balance" it. The hands should remain steady in your pattern and not moving up or down in an effort to balance the shell. As the great Australian coach, Steve Fairbairn, instructed his crews, "Don't let your rigger rise".

The Entry for a sweep rower is, perhaps, more difficult than for a sculler. In the first place, the boat is generally moving faster and, therefore, your movements must be relatively quicker. Nonetheless, it is still necessary to respect the same principles of geometry and physics. Continuing the angular rotation of your trunk around the pin, follow the arc of the handle. Continue to use your inside arm to propel yourself into the stern, not the legs.

As the inside arm continues to apply pressure against the pin into the blade, push the blade into the water with the outside arm. As in sculling, your entire core is engaged onto the rigger. In other words, the inside arm propels you into the stern and the outside arm places the blade into the water. Simply put, do not fly "up and out"!

Once again, there is no "instantaneous" beginning of the Drive. You must allow Bernoulli to sink his teeth into the blade. There is still that moment, albeit now even briefer, of Dead Time, before driving off the foot stretcher, while the blade is loading. As in sculling, this moment is ultimately from whence the boat's speed is going to come.

The Drive differs from sculling in that you emphasize the leverage advantage of the outside arm throughout most of Drive except for just before the Release when the inside arm is working strongly against the pin and the outside arm is transitioning from the draw into the Release/Follow-Through. As with sculling, it is important to always be attuned to the subtle changes of your relationship to the pin and the vector related to the movement of the blade through the water.

In general, as with sculling, you are always applying constant pressure against the pin in the direction of the movement of the blade. At the back end of the Drive/front end of the Recovery, the pressure is directed toward the blade, which is in the stern. As you swing forward, the vector is constantly shifting and becomes more "lateral" and, finally, it shifts toward the bow.

At the back end of the Drive, while still using your outside arm to draw the handle toward your body, the emphasis shifts slightly to the inside arm, which should be pushing the button firmly against the pin toward the blade. Just as at the Entry, there is a division of labor at the Release between outside and inside arms; whereas at the Entry it was the inside arm pushing against the pin and the outside arm placing the blade in the water, at the Release it is the inside arm pushing against the pin and the outside arm levering the oar out of the water. The shift becomes obvious and natural if we are always thinking in terms of pressure against the pin.

U.S. Olympic Eight Showing Shell Velocity as a Function of Time
(Taken from Martin and Bernfield, **Medicine and Science in Sports and Exercise, 1980**)

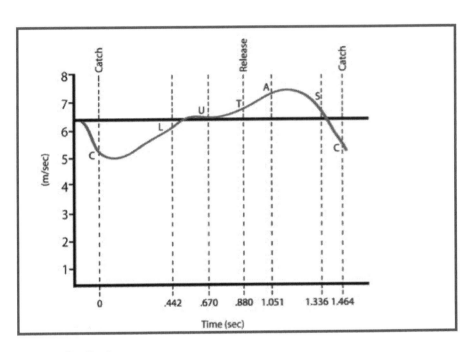

C = Catch
CL = Leg Drive
LU = Upper Body Drive
UT = Transition
TA = Hands and Upper Body Away
AS = Seat Movement
SC = Blade to Water

The Velocity Curve above is courtsy of Martin and Bernfield, **Medicine and Science in Sports and Exercise, 1980.**

The Velocity Curve Diagrams **(pages: 5, 9, 14, 21, 29)** appear courtsy of Wenzel Joesten, Berlin, Germany.

Note the similarity of the velocity curve of an Olympic Eight and our velocity curve of a single sculler (pages 5, 9, 14, 21, and 29).

Velocity curves of all our shells, 1x, 2x, 4x, 2+, and 2-, 4+ and 4- and 8+ are all essentially the same except for the speed of the boat.

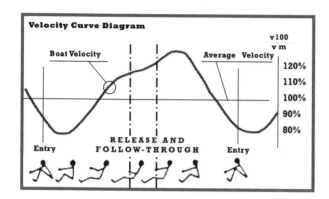

Velocity Curve Diagram

Notes

Notes

Notes

Notes

Notes

Notes

Gordon has more than three decades of university, national, and international coaching experience. His university coaching has included MIT Head Men's Heavyweight coach for 20 years, Williams College, and University of Virginia.

He has coached US women's sweep and sculling national teams at the World Championships, Goodwill Games, and World University Games, in addition to international crews from Peru (World Championships and Pan American Games), Puerto Rico (Central American and Caribbean Games), and Brazil (Olympic Trials). Gordon is regularly a guest coach at Cambridge University Women's Crew (England), Open Water Rowing Club (CA), Craftsbury Sculling Center (VT), and has coached at both Cambridge Boat Club and Riverside Boat Club in Cambridge Ma..

Gordon was educated at Columbia University and Cambridge University—where he rowed for 1st & 3rd Trinity. He is currently chief coach at the Florida Rowing Center and an independent sculling coach. Gordon lives in Belmont, Ma. and Wellington, Fl.

39716492R00059

Made in the USA
San Bernardino, CA
02 October 2016